Shotokan Karate

SHOTOKAN KARATE

Ashley Croft

The Crowood Press

First published in 2001 by
The Crowood Press Ltd
Ramsbury, Marlborough
Wiltshire SN8 2HR

© Ashley Croft 2001

British Library Cataloguing-in-Publication Data
A catalogue record for this book is available from the British Library.

ISBN 1 86126 390 2

Photography by Martin Baugh

Dedication
I dedicate this book to my wife Karen and children Alex and Daniel,
for their undying support.

Typeset by Phoenix Typesetting, Ilkley, West Yorkshire

Printed and bound in Great Britain by J W Arrowsmith, Bristol

Contents

CONTENTS

CONTENTS

Acknowledgements

There are many people who have influenced my karate over the years to whom I am eternally indebted and would like to extend my thanks and appreciation.

First, there is Sensei Paul Evans who introduced me to karate and more than wetted my appetite while working in the Sultanate of Oman in the late 1970s. I would also like to thank Senseis John Van Weenan and Robin Reid who have both provided me with a good technical grounding.

In more recent times, I owe my gratitude to Senseis John Flavell and Archie Fieldhouse. Both are excellent exponents of Shotokan karate and have a deep passion for the art that cannot fail to rub off on those who have the good fortune of meeting and training with them. When I enter the dojo for a training session under John and Archie it is fair to say that I never know what to expect other than I can guarantee I will depart having acquired a further golden nugget to store away for prosperity. They have both had a major influence on my overall karate philosophy – for John and Archie, karate really has become a way of life.

I have also had the great fortune of being able to train under Professor Rick Clark, a truly talented martial artist who has opened up my mind to new horizons and given me further direction in my own quest to find the way. Among other things, one important lesson I have learnt from Rick is that no particular martial art is better than the next – each style has its own strengths, and a true martial artist will come to understand and embrace this concept.

Last, but far from least, I would like to thank those close to me. Many of the karateka that I have had the pleasure of teaching over the years have become good friends and contributed to my own personal development. However, I would like to single out Craig Jones, Erin Thwaites, Robin Thwaites, Steve Southwood, Helen Southwood and Judy Hyland for their help in preparing this book and for agreeing to feature in some of the photographs.

You have given me great inspiration, aspiration and support for which I sincerely thank you all.

Ashley Croft

Forewords

**By John Flavell (6th Dan) and
Archie Fieldhouse (5th Dan)**

As martial artists with over thirty years of experience we are acutely aware of the dedication and skill required to achieve the highest levels of understanding of martial technique. We are equally aware that many so-called dedicated students of martial arts fall by the wayside, without ever managing to scale the dizzy heights of technical enlightenment.

So too is Ashley Croft, a karateka as skilful and dedicated as any we have come across in all our years of training together. Since he is blessed with such qualities in abundance, coupled with great perception and in-exhaustible patience, it will come as no surprise to discover that he is chief instructor and guiding light to the very successful Chiltern Karate Association.

Having first met Ashley some seven or eight years ago it was instantly obvious that this thoroughly likeable gentlemen has a deep love for his chosen art and a thirst for knowledge that knows no bounds. His under-standing of the principles and ethics of Shotokan karate are none more evident than when you walk into one of his dojos and witness the remarkable standard of his students, their outstanding enthusiasm, and the excellent etiquette that this natural leader has instilled into them.

We have always found Ashley to be a very personable, approachable individual who possesses an air of assured self-confidence, and having seen at first hand the way he conducts himself and his association, we have no doubts that he will go on from success to success. The idea that he should want to write a book about karate is absolutely typical of the nature of the man, a reflection of his deep desire to understand and then pass on that understanding to others.

Ashley has stated that every time he trains with us he always takes away a 'golden nugget of knowledge to preserve for prosperity'. The truth of the matter is that Ashley himself is the golden nugget and each time we train together we just polish that nugget a little brighter.

By Professor Rick Clark (8th Dan)

I have been training in the martial arts since 1962 and have had the good fortune of meeting fellow martial artists in many countries around the world. I have known Ashley Croft for a number of years and find him to be a skilled and intelligent martial artist. We first met on my initial tours of the UK, and since that time he has been an active

11

supporter of my seminars and hosts me on a regular basis in his clubs.

I have always been impressed by his passion for karate and thirst for knowledge to increase the skills and abilities of his students and himself. To me, the desire to further the knowledge and skills of your students is the foremost duty of an instructor. I have been very pleased that Ashley Croft is of like mind. To this end he has always been very open minded in his approach to karate, resulting in a substantial depth of knowledge developed over many years. I know that this book has been written in partial fulfilment of his fervent desire to pass on this knowledge to fellow karateka.

The book is unique in that it provides detailed theory and explanation of the karate techniques but presented in a manner that can be easily followed and understood by all, regardless of grade and level of experience. It is comprehensive and meticulous and contains a depth of material unsurpassed in a book of this nature.

The material contained in the following pages will be invaluable for both those just starting off in karate and for the more senior student. It provides an excellent reference guide for all those in search of excellence.

I proudly associate myself with this publication and highly recommend it to all traditional karate students.

By Craig Jones (3rd Dan)

Initially, although extremely honoured, I was somewhat surprised when approached to write a foreword for this book. But, as with all things that Ashley embarks upon, the reason is in fact perfectly clear.

As a young man in the early 1970s I was drawn to the martial arts via judo, and have had the opportunity to train with a number of inspirational instructors from various 'styles' on and off ever since. I became involved with Shotokan in the 1980s and, after a short period of absence, joined a newly formed karate club in my local town. This is when I was first introduced to Ashley Croft, and with over ten years of his unique tuition quite literally 'under my belt', I think it is fair to say my karate is quite simply the product of his dynamic instruction, in-depth knowledge and constant guidance.

Within the martial arts there are a number of truly dedicated instructors with the rare qualities of enthusiasm, dedication and ability that are so vital in the search for perfection within their particular fields. These are the people travelling along 'their way' while embracing and adapting to actively research the true meanings of the ancient fighting arts. Ashley Croft is one such man.

Needless to say, not all these talented individuals have written books and therefore there are few comprehensive, quality publications that actually manage to convey effectively to the reader how and why various karate techniques should be delivered.

You may have, as I have, sat in front of videos in freeze-frame mode or squinted at books from past masters where a kata or a technique is depicted wondering 'why is their foot there . . . how did the hands end up there . . . what is the application of that technique?' The material that makes up the contents of this book serves effectively to enlighten the reader, not confuse still further.

Although it is true to say there are other karate books available on the market, there are none with the same degree of detail and 'real life' experience as contained in this publication. I have never come across a book that not only demonstrates how to do things correctly but also shows the most common faults and how to avoid them.

I know this book is born from Ashley Croft's constant desire to impart his knowledge and experience, and while not intended to substitute dojo instruction it is a 'must' in any serious traditional karate practitioner's library.

I have had the pleasure and direct benefit of Sensei Croft's 'hands-on' instruction: this book is the very best next thing.

13

Preface

I am very much a perfectionist when it comes to my own karate, always striving to improve and further develop my knowledge and skills. When I first started training I sought technical perfection in everything I did and had an unquenchable thirst for further knowledge. To that end I spent many hours and wore out numerous pairs of shoes walking from bookshop to bookshop searching for the material that would give me the knowledge that I was seeking. More often than not, I came away disappointed and empty handed.

Although I found there were many karate books on the market, some very good and others not so good, I could not find one that covered the techniques that I was being taught with sufficient explanation. It was on one of these occasions, having disappointedly toured the bookshops, that I decided to prepare a book to help others following in my footsteps.

I have therefore written this book to assist karateka at all levels to develop their own knowledge of the technical aspects of the karate techniques they are taught in the dojo. It is hoped that it will assist the many karateka who have the dedication and drive to put in the extra hours of research and training necessary to satisfy their thirst for knowledge. Whether just commencing karate or preparing for senior grades, it is hoped that some benefit will be derived from this text.

I believe that it should be a prerequisite for students wishing to progress to senior grade and ultimately black belt level that they should have a good understanding of what they are doing and why. This principle is fundamental and if it is not followed closely, the quality of karate will slowly degenerate. The students of today will become the instructors of tomorrow and be responsible for spreading the 'way' of karate.

This book should be used to supplement training and to enhance knowledge and skills. It is intended for reference purposes and is not a substitute for the many hours of hard work that must be put in to make satisfactory progress in this fascinating art.

Good luck in your endeavours.

Ashley Croft

1 Introduction

There has always been a degree of mystique behind karate, possibly due to the fact that for centuries it has been taught in secret, surrounded by folklore and anecdotes of superhuman feats performed by past masters. This has been further fuelled in more recent times through the array of martial art based films where wood or brick breaking techniques are demonstrated to the amazement of audiences all around the world. Unfortunately, this has resulted in false perceptions being formed as to what karate is all about. People starting this fascinating art will find that there are few secrets, all it takes to progress is a will to succeed, hard work and perseverance.

In fact, the hardest step anyone takes in karate is summing up the courage to enter the dojo (training hall) for the first time, not really knowing what will happen or what surprises are in store. Good karate clubs will recognize the difficulties and concerns that face beginners and offer a friendly, nurturing environment in which everyone is made to feel welcome. Karate should be for everyone, young and old, male and female. Instructors have a responsibility to their students and should steer clear of macho-based training methods that deter people who have the potential to be good

karateka, but never take that decisive first step.

After training for a short period of time it will become apparent that karate is by no means easy and its intricacies will take many years to perfect, if perfection is at all possible. Steady progression will take a great deal of resolve, determination and persistence but will bring with it great personal satisfaction and reward. In time it will go beyond the physical, karate will truly become a way of life.

When first starting on a training programme, keep in mind that each individual is different and unique; some people will be naturally strong, others more flexible. Do not be overly concerned about making comparisons with others, instead concentrate on developing self-discipline and work hard to improve oneself and reduce areas of weakness.

At times, improvement will be slow and therefore not easily measured, which may result in periods of despondency. However, it is worth remembering that improvement is often made in small increments, but that this will eventually result in quite significant progression.

I believe that one of the contributory factors to dismay and despondency is modern training methods that require students to achieve so much in such a short period of time, placing them under undue pressure. The grading system and the desire to move quickly through the grades can aggravate this. In your own interests be aware and wary of these pressures. If the going gets tough remind yourself that there is no substitute for time in the search for proficiency of technique. Students of the past often spent three years and more practising a single kata and were not permitted by their senseis to move on until it had been mastered. There is an Okinawan maxim 'mukin shori' that encapsulates this. When translated it means 'the way to success has no short cuts'.

Sensei Gichin Funakoshi, the founder of Shotokan karate, once wrote that karate is not about victory or defeat but about the perfection of character. You will come to understand this in time and realize that grade is not important.

The following chapters provide a comprehensive coverage of traditional karate training methods and important fundamental concepts, together with a detailed analysis of the basic karate techniques.

On a final note, remember:

The boundaries of human achievement lie only in the mind.

Shoshin Nagamine

2 The History and Development of Karate

The evolution of karate is shrouded in mystery and its exact origins have never been established with any degree of certainty. The lack of available information can be attributed to the fact that historically karate was taught behind closed doors, with past masters tending to pass on their secrets verbally to a trusted few disciples. What limited written material there was suffered the effects of the battle for Okinawa during the Second World War and much was destroyed. To piece together the history of karate, reliance must now be placed on archaeological discoveries, historical documents where available, a degree of folklore, and accounts of past events that have been passed down by word of mouth through successive generations in Okinawa.

Methods of unarmed combat have been practised for thousands of years. This is evidenced by very significant archaeological discoveries, made in 1839, during excavations in Mesopotamia (now Iraq). During these excavations, the British antiquarian and diplomat, Sir Henry Austen Layard, uncovered a buried library belonging to King Assurbanipal of the Assyrian Empire (668–626BC). A substantial amount of carved tablets were recovered from the site over a number of years, which together with others discovered in the region have enabled the legendary Epic of Gilgamesh to be pieced together.

Gilgamesh was the King of Urak in Babylonia in about 2500BC, and the carved tablets describe him as a great warrior and exponent of armed and unarmed combat. They also describe how wrestling matches and trials of strength were conducted between warrior-youths. Although these tablets provide good evidence to suggest that Gilgamesh was quite an adept martial artist, it has not been possible to establish the extent of his mastery of these arts, or any link between him and the martial arts as we know them today. What is interesting is that the Epic of Gilgamesh does show early development of systematic methods of unarmed self-defence and adds to the mysteries of the origins of modern karate.

In order to examine what is actually known with any degree of certainty, it is necessary to move on some 3,900 years from Gilgamesh and Mesopotamia to the Far East and the island of Okinawa. Okinawa is a small island located in the East China Sea, 500 miles south of Japan (Fig 1). Due to its strategic position, it has had to suffer a succession of invasions and periods of oppression over many years. In 1477, following a period of political turbulence, the King of Okinawa, Sho Shin, banned the carrying of weapons by any of the inhabitants. In 1609 the island was invaded by the Japanese who continued to enforce this ban by barring the carrying of weapons by anyone other than samurai.

As a result of this policy, the islanders secretly developed systems of unarmed combat that became known as Okinawan-te, the word 'te' meaning hands. (This is sometimes referred to as just 'te' or 'tode'.) Over the ensuing years the Okinawan-te developed into three distinct styles around the main towns of Naha, Shuri and Tomari (Fig 2).

These styles became known simply as Naha-te, Shuri-te and Tomari-te.

The names have changed in more recent years with Naha-te developing into Gojo-ryu (the hard and soft school) which is how it is still known today, while Shuri-te and Tomari-te merged, in the late nineteenth century, under the name Shorin-ryu. It is from Shorin-ryu that Shotokan karate, one of the most widely practised styles today, has developed.

In the late nineteenth century, the karate masters agreed the name karate should be used to encompass all the styles with the original ideogram for the word meaning 'China hand'. This was later changed so that the word karate translated as 'empty hand', making it more acceptable to the Japanese.

One of the most influential figures in the development of modern-day karate was Sensei Gichin Funakoshi. He was born in

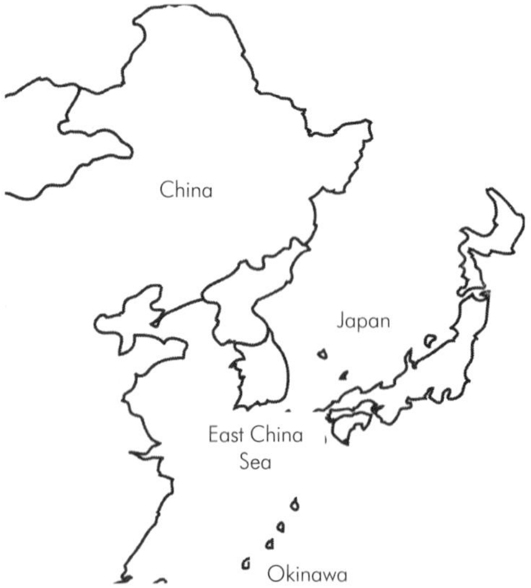

Fig 1 The East China Sea region

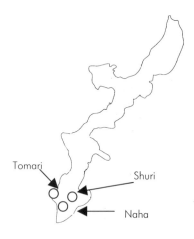

Fig 2 The island of Okinawa

Okinawa on 10 November 1868 in the village of Yamakawa on the outskirts of the town of Shuri. He started learning karate from an early age and devoted his whole life to his beloved art. He commenced his training in Okinawa under two renowned and formidable martial artists, Masters Anko Azato (1827–1906), and Anko Itosu (1813–1915) of whom he describes great feats in his autobiography *Karate-do, My Way of Life*. Itosu was a great reformer and creator of kata, leaving as his legacy the heian (pinan) kata as well some of the more advanced forms including tekki nidan, tekki sandan, kanku sho and bassai sho.

At the age of twenty, Sensei Funakoshi took up teaching and spent thirty years of his life teaching in schools around Shuri and Naha. Throughout this time he continued to train tirelessly in karate under the watchful eye of Masters Azato and Itosu.

Shortly after retiring from teaching he was responsible for introducing karate into Japan – in 1915 he and others gave a demonstration of karate at the judo headquarters in Tokyo. This demonstration generated a great deal of interest resulting in Sensei Funakoshi remaining in Japan to teach his art. Subsequently many other Okinawan masters followed in his footsteps and, in a very short space of time, karate was being practised in all corners of the country.

In 1936 Sensei Funakoshi established the Shotokan training school in Tokyo, from which Shotokan karate derives its name. 'Shoto' means waving pines, a pen name he used when writing poetry, and 'kan' means hall.

It is possible to trace the roots of modern karate back with a fair degree of accuracy to the early 1700s. We know that Azato and Itosu, both of whom followed the Shuri-te lineage, influenced Funakoshi's karate. They, in turn, were both taught by 'Bushi' Matsumura Sokon who studied under 'Toudi' Sukagawa. Sukagawa was a prominent martial artist in Okinawa and is believed to have spent time studying the fighting systems in China. It is also believed that he received instruction from the Chinese Military Attaché, to Okinawa, Kushanku (after whom the kata kanku dai is named). It is known that Itosu also received instruction in Tomari-te under Kasaku Matsunura. The genealogy of karate from Funakoshi can be traced with accuracy back to the early 1700s (Fig 3).

The further back in time one goes, the more clouded events become. Nevertheless, there is significant evidence to show that the Okinawan martial arts were influenced by the early fighting arts of China. It is known that trade routes existed between Okinawa and China at the time that Okinawan-te was undergoing its development, and that diplomatic relations existed, with the exchange of ambassadors between the two countries.

Further evidence of the Chinese influence can be found in the karate kata, examples being the kata kanku dai and chinte. As stated above, kanku dai was originally named after its creator Kushanku, while chinte (Chinese hands) is believed to have deep Chinese origins. Furthermore, the kata jion, jitte and ji'in all commence with a Chinese salutation 'jiai no kamae'.

The fighting arts of China can be traced back to the early sixth century and it is

19

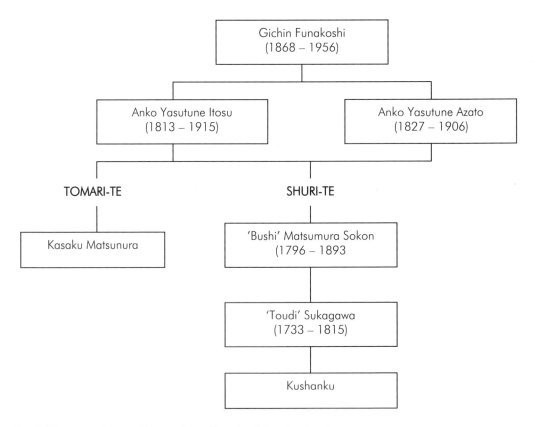

Fig 3 The genealogy of karate from Funakoshi to Kushanku

believed they were strongly influenced by Buddhism, in particular the teachings of an Indian monk named Bodhidarma.

The birthplace of Buddhism was in the foothills of the Himalayan Mountains in northern India. Its founder was Siddhartha Gautama, born around 566BC, who became known as the Buddha (the enlightened one). Buddhism spread quickly throughout India and was imported into China during the first century AD by Indian merchants and monks who travelled the silk roads.

Bodhidarma is known to have spent many years teaching the monks of the Shaolin monastery, which is located in the Songshan mountains in the Kingdom of Wei, northern China (Fig 4). The Shaolin monastery is so named because of its position within a small forest, 'shao' meaning small and 'lin' meaning wood.

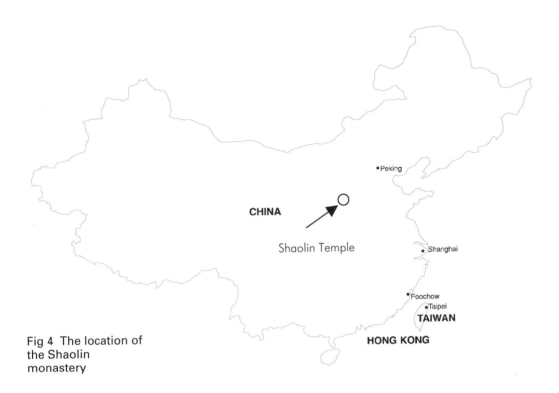

Fig 4 The location of
the Shaolin
monastery

As well as teaching Buddhism within the monastery, Bodhidarma provided the Shaolin monks with instruction in breathing and fighting skills. Interestingly, India has its own indigenous martial art called Kalaripayit, which in its original form may have inspired Bodhidarma.

Although karate, like all other things, has had to change over the years, its fundamental principles have stood the test of time. Today, students of the art will practise many of the techniques as they were taught hundreds of years ago.

If a holistic view is taken of events as described above it is possible that the karate practised today is linked back through Okinawa to China and the Shaolin monastery. However, the further back one goes the more tenuous the links become – who knows, we may also be following in the footsteps of the great man Gilgamesh himself!

21

3 The Foundations of Karate

When first selecting a club or association to join, consideration should be given to the training methods employed and what the overall aims, objectives and philosophy of the club are. Most traditional karate clubs will have a structured approach to the lessons in which training is broken down into three areas – kihon (basic techniques), kumite (sparring) and kata (pre-arranged forms). These are described in more detail below. A good club will have a well-balanced syllabus with equal weighting between the three areas that should not be viewed in isolation, as separate disciplines, but linked to form a complete system.

Kihon (Basic Techniques)

This is where the basic blocks, kicks, punches, strikes and stances are taught. Instruction will commence with fairly simple moves and become more and more advanced with progression. Many of the moves taught will feel alien to the body and must be performed slowly at first, only applying speed and power when the body can cope without suffering undue injury. This book is primarily concerned with providing detailed explana-

tion and instruction in these basic techniques, highlighting the main areas of difficulty commonly experienced.

There is a lot more to learning the basic techniques than first meets the eye. As well as the actual mechanics of the moves, other physical and mental aspects need to be considered. Sensei Gichin Funakoshi described three cardinal points that should always be borne in mind during karate practice: light and heavy application of strength, expansion and contraction of the body, and fast and slow movements in techniques. In executing karate techniques, whether it is during basic training, kumite or kata, these various elements must be considered. For example, when blocking only use as much power as is necessary to succeed and then counter-attack with full speed and power with correct focus. All too often brute force is relied upon to the neglect of correct body action and timing.

Whatever the karate technique being performed, the method of delivery should not vary between basics, kumite or kata. For example, if someone has a strong, powerful mae geri (front kick) when paired up in kumite then the quality of the kick should not change in the performance of kata or when training in basics. Unfortunately it is all too often the case that quality varies considerably between the disciplines.

Kumite (Sparring)

Kumite is the sparring element, which comes in a number of forms ranging from pre-arranged sets of attacks and blocks to freestyle fighting, which allows the use of any technique. During the early stages of training, only basic sparring will be undertaken in controlled circumstances: this is to reduce the likelihood of injury.

Gohon Kumite (Five-Step Sparring)

In gohon kumite one side attacks the other while stepping forward five times, usually in zenkutsu dachi (front stance). The attacks can vary, traditionally between jodan (upper-level), chudan (mid-level) and mae geri (front kick). When the attacks are jodan, the blocks should be age uke (upper rising block); soto ude uke (outside forearm block) defends against chudan attack and the mae geri is countered by gedan barai (downward block). Of course, with a little imagination the method of attack and defence can be varied.

Both partners commence the sequence facing each other in yoi (ready position). The person nominated to do the attacking sequence first will then step back with the right foot performing a downward block in front stance. For kicking attacks the start varies slightly with both hands held out to the side as fists.

The attacker then carries out the five attacks, stepping forward each time, with kiai (a loud shout) on the fifth move. The defender when blocking steps back each time and counter-attacks after the final block with a gyaku zuki (reverse punch) and should kiai at this point. At the end of the five moves and on the command yame (stop), both sides should step into yoi with the attacker stepping backward and the defender forward. The whole sequence should then be repeated so at the end both persons have attacked and defended in the same way.

Sanbon Kumite (Three-Step Sparring)

This is three-step sparring in which the attack changes with each step. The sequence commences from the gedan barai position, in the same way as gohon kumite, but in this case should be practised starting from both left and right stances.

The first attack is jodan, the second chudan and the third, final move mae geri. The defender, while stepping back, blocks with age uke, soto ude uke and gedan barai countering with gyaku zuki and kiai.

Kaeshi Ippon Kumite (Returning One-Step Sparring)

In this method of sparring both parties attack and defend in turn using a variety of attacking and defending techniques. The sequence commences with both sides standing in yoi facing each other. The person nominated to attack first will then step back into the gedan barai position. Using a punching sequence as an example, the attacker steps forward and attacks with a punch to the head that is defended with an age uke while stepping back. The defender (the one doing the age uke) then attacks back immediately, stepping forward with a punch to the stomach, which is defended with soto ude uke/gyaku zuki while stepping back. Both sides then pull back into yoi and the moves are repeated alternating who does the first attack.

Kihon Ippon Kumite (One-Step Sparring)

This form of sparring involves single attacks that include both punches and kicks. The attacks commence from the gedan barai position for the punching techniques and from zenkutsu dachi with the hands at the side for the kicks. After each attack the attacker must step back to the start position before undertaking the next move.

In kihon ippon kumite the defender can block and counter-attack in many different ways and it differs from gohon and sanbon kumite in that the defences are not all back in a straight line but include side-stepping at angles to evade and deflect incoming attacks.

Jiyu Ippon Kumite (Semi-Freestyle Sparring)

As with kihon ippon kumite, jiyu ippon involves single attacks using both punches and kicks. Both attack and defence commence from a freestyle stance. Jiyu ippon techniques tend to be shorter, snappier and faster resembling a more freestyle approach.

Okuri Jiyu Ippon (Sparring with Two Consecutive Attacks)

This is now moving close to full freestyle sparring. Both attacker and defender face one another in a freestyle stance. The move starts with the attacker stepping in with a pre-determined attack. This is blocked and counter-attacked. As soon as the counter-attack is complete the original attacker follows up with a second attack that can be any punch, strike or kick. The defender should again block and counter-attack to complete the move.

Jiyu Kumite (Freestyle Sparring)

Freestyle sparring enables all karate techniques to be practised with a partner. This provides the environment in which any technique can be used in any sequence or combination. For safety reasons, some techniques are frowned upon: these include elbow strikes, kicks to the head using the ball of the foot and open-handed strikes.

General Considerations

If any injury is going to occur in karate it is usually during kumite practice. If controlled properly and due respect is afforded to one another, such injuries should be few and far between. It is also important that the instructor's commands are adhered to at all times.

When practising any type of kumite for the first time, commence slowly and only build up speed and power as ability and confidence permits. The following points should always be taken into consideration:

1. Include realism – kumite is the closest that most people will come to a combat situation so it must include a high level of realism. When attacking at high speed

do so with conviction and spirit, making sure that the technique will work.

2. Use correct technique – always endeavour to use correct karate techniques when attacking and defending.
3. Body movement – strive to ensure fluidity of movement when attacking and defending, concentrating on tai sabaki (correct body movement) and ashi sabaki (foot movement).
4. Distancing – in both attack and defence ensure that maai (correct distance) is maintained.
5. Correct application of power – only use as much force as is necessary to achieve the desired result.
6. Aiming points – concentrate on the aiming points when directing attacks and counter-attacks.

Kata (Forms)

Kata consist of a number of different prearranged defensive and offensive movements against imaginary opponents and form an important part of training. It is from the serious study of kata that the ability will be developed to deliver a strike or block in any direction against multiple attacks. It is this ability that makes karate such an effective form of self-defence. The Shotokan style of karate has twenty-nine kata which consist of the three taikyoku kata, five heian kata and twenty-one more advanced forms. A full list, including their original Okinawan names and origins, is included in Appendix II.

There are three stages of learning a kata. First it is necessary to master the moves and pattern of the kata. The next stage is to work towards performing the kata with correct application of speed, timing, power and fluidity of movement. The third and higher stage of learning is to take the kata apart and understand the bunkai (application) of each move, including the target areas. This stage of learning will naturally include the kyusho (pressure point) applications. Sadly, most people fail to move forward to this stage of learning.

To derive maximum benefit from kata performance at this stage, the mind must be focused on the task at hand and the purpose of each move. To achieve this, the imaginary opponent and the mode of attack must be visualized at all times. Once this stage of learning has been achieved, the kata will come to life and can be performed with meaning, feeling and spirit. Consider it as a personal battle against deadly adversaries from which only one victor can emerge.

Masatoshi Nakayama describes six specific points that must be borne in mind when performing kata. These build on Sensei Funakoshi's three cardinal point theory (*see* page 22).

Nakayama's Six Points of Kata

1. Correct order – the number and sequence of movements are predetermined and all must be performed.
2. Beginning and end – the kata must begin and end at the same spot on the embusen (the performance line of the kata).
3. Meaning of each movement – each movement, defensive or offensive, must be clearly understood and fully expressed.
4. Awareness of the target – the karateka

must know what the target is and precisely when to execute a technique.

5. Rhythm and timing – rhythm must be appropriate to the particular kata and the body must be flexible, never over-strained. Always keep in mind three factors: correct use of power, swiftness or slowness in executing techniques, and the stretching and contracting of muscles.

6. Proper breathing – breathing should adjust to changing situations, but basically inhale when blocking, exhale when executing a finishing technique, and inhale and exhale while executing successive techniques.

Closely related to breathing is the kiai (loud shout) coming in the middle or at the end of the kata, at the moment of maximum tension. By exhaling very sharply and tensing the abdomen, extra power can be imparted to the muscles.

Japanese Customs

Although the origins of karate can be traced back over hundreds of years from Okinawa to China, it is the Japanese that have had the greatest influence on its development in more recent years. This has resulted in Japanese being adopted as the international language of karate, and a number of Japanese customs have become an intrinsic part of the art. A comprehensive list of Japanese terminology and the commands used in the dojo are included in the Terminology section (see page 213) – the more frequently used customs are outlined below.

Oss

Oss is a Japanese word often used among karate practitioners. It has many meanings from a basic greeting to an acknowledgement of understanding. It is also used to express respect to fellow karateka and must be spoken positively with spirit and sincerity.

Rei (Bow)

Although alien to Western cultures, the bow is an important part of the karate etiquette. It is used to establish a relationship of respect and trust between karateka and should be accompanied by the word 'oss'. Sensei Funakoshi enshrined the importance of the bow in his twenty precepts of karate in which he stated 'karate begins and ends with a bow'. His precepts are reproduced at the end of this chapter and it is recommended that they be given careful consideration.

To perform the bow correctly, commence in heisoku dachi (informal attention stance) with the hands open and placed on the side of the legs (some associations use musubi dachi, also an informal attention stance, in which to perform the bow). Lean forward, bending at the waist, to an angle of about 30 degrees, at the same time saying 'oss'. Hold the bow at this point for a couple of seconds and then return to the upright position. A more detailed explanation of the bow from the standing position as described above, and the seiza (sitting position) is provided in Chapter 5.

Kiai

The kiai is a loud shout that is used to demonstrate martial spirit and the combined physical and spiritual energy. It must be shouted using the tanden or hara in the lower abdomen and shouted with feeling and conviction. At least one kiai, normally two, appear at set points in the kata. It should also be used when attacking and counter-attacking in kumite and at set points in basics.

Dojo Kun

The dojo kun contains the rules of the dojo and is often recited at the end of lessons as part of a formal ceremony. It is said that the Okinawan Master Sakugawa Shungo first introduced these rules and that he based them on a Chinese dojo kun originating from Bodhidharma and the Shaolin monastery. It is traditional for the sempai (senior student) to recite each line, which is repeated in turn by the other karateka present. At the conclusion shomen ni rei (a formal bow to the front) is performed which is followed by sensei ni rei (a bow to the sensei). The dojo kun is likely to be performed more frequently in the traditional karate clubs and associations.

Dojo Kun
1. Hitotsu, jinkaku kansei ni tsutomuru koto.
2. Hitotsu, makoto no michi o mamoru koto.
3. Hitotsu, doryoku no seishin o yashinau koto.
4. Hitotsu, reigi o omonzuru koto.
5. Hitotsu, kekki no yu o imashimuru koto.

SKI Translation
1. One, to strive for the perfection of character!
2. One, to defend the path of truth!
3. One, to foster the spirit of effort!
4. One, to honour the principles of etiquette!
5. One, to guard against impetuous courage!

JKA (Japan Karate Association) Translation
1. Seek perfection of character
2. Be faithful
3. Endeavour
4. Respect others
5. Refrain from violent behaviour

The dojo kun is performed in seiza (sitting position). The process of moving into and out of the seiza position is explained in Chapter 5.

Funakoshi's Precepts of Karate

Sensei Funakoshi (1868–1957) had a major influence on the development and spread of modern-day karate. He was the founder of the Shotokan style of karate and the first chief instructor of the Japanese Karate Association (JKA). One of his legacies to karateka of today and the future are his twenty precepts of karate that are reproduced below.

1. Karate wa rei ni hajimari rei ni owaru koto o wasureru na.
   (Never forget karate begins and ends with rei. Rei has the meaning of courtesy and respect.)
2. Karate ne sente nashi.
   (There is no first attack in karate.)
3. Karate wa gi no tasuke.
   (Karate supports righteousness.)

4. Mazu jiko o shire shikoshite hoka o shire.
   (First understand yourself, then understand others.)
5. Gijutsu yori shinjutsu.
   (The art of mind is more important than the art of technique.)
6. Kokoro wa hanatan koto o yosu.
   (The mind needs to be freed.)
7. Wazawai wa ketai ni shozu.
   (Trouble is born of negligence.)
8. Dojo nami no karate to omou na.
   (Do not think that karate is only in the dojo.)
9. Karate no shugyo wa issho dearu.
   (The training of karate requires a lifetime.)
10. Arayuru mono o karateka se soko ni myomi ari.
    (Transform everything into karate; there lies the exquisiteness.)
11. Karate wa yu no gotoku taezu netsu o ataezareba moto no mizu ni kaeru.
    (Genuine karate is like hot water; it cools down if you do not keep on heating it.)
12. Katsu kangae wa motsu na makenu kangae wa hitsuyo.
    (Do not have an idea of winning, while the idea of not losing is necessary.)
13. Teki ni yotte tenka seyo.
    (Transform yourself according to the opponent.)
14. Ikusa wa kyojitsu no soju ikan ni ari.
    (The outcome of the fight all depends on manoeuvre.)
15. Hito no teashi o ken to omoe.
    (Imagine one's arms and legs as swords.)
16. Danshi mon o izureba hyakuman no teki ari.
    (Once you leave the shelter of home, there are a million enemies.)
17. Kamae wa shoshinsha ni, ato wa shizentai.
    (Postures are for the beginner; later they are natural positions.)
18. Kata wa tadashiku, jissen wa betsumoso.
    (Do the kata correctly; the real fight is a different matter.)
19. Chikara no kyojaku, karada no shinshuku, waza no kankyo o wasureru na.
    (Do not forget the control of the dynamics of power, the elasticity of body and the speed of technique.)
20. Tsune ni shinenkofu seyo.
    (Always be good at the application of everything that you have learned.)

Grading Structure

Grades up to black belt are referred to as 'kyu' grades and a different coloured belt identifies each grade. There are ten grades up to black belt and it will normally take about four years to progress to this level. The coloured belt given to each kyu grade varies from club to club, although the actual kyu grade remains consistent. 10th kyu will be the first grade and 1st kyu the senior. Some associations employ a system of intermediate grades for junior students, aimed at ensuring a good grounding in the basic techniques and kata before the more advanced applications. An example of a typical grading syllabus is included in Appendix I.

Training Aids

The forbears of modern karate made use of many articles to aid their training and physical development. These included chisi (a stick with a heavy weight on one end), kami (heavy earthen jars), makiwara (striking boards) and ishi-geta (stone clogs). Sensei Gichin Funakoshi is known to have regularly worn heavy clogs to strengthen his legs. Fortunately, modern training aids are not quite so primitive.

Once a reasonable level of competence has been achieved, it is advisable to practise punching, striking and kicking a heavy training bag. Start off slowly to avoid injury, building up speed and power as confidence grows. Including bag work in the training routine is a must for senior grades.

Ankle and wrist weights can be used to help strengthen the arms and legs. Virtually all karate techniques can be performed while wearing the weights. This should be done slowly for greatest benefit.

Flexibility training can be aided by a variety of stretching machines and devices. The benefit of these is that advanced stretching exercises can be undertaken without the assistance of a partner.

Levels of the Body

For the purpose of describing target areas the body is divided into three levels that will often be referred to. These are jodan (upper-level), chudan (mid-level) and gedan (lower-level) (Fig 5).

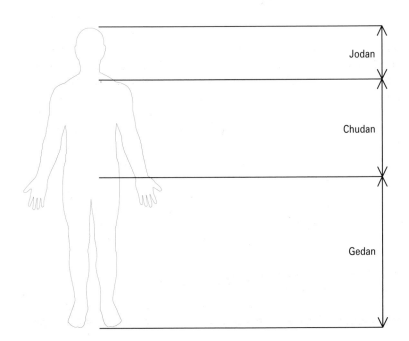

Fig 5 The three levels of the body

Warm-Up Exercises

All lessons will commence with a warm-up and conclude with a cool-down period. The warm-up will aim to concentrate on the whole body, paying particular attention to the muscle groups that will be used during the lesson and those that require flexibility training for the various kicks, strikes and blocks. The warm-up and cool-down are necessary to prevent injury or muscle pain. The subject of flexibility training is dealt with in more detail in Chapter 9.

Fitness

Although karate is first and foremost a martial art, it is also a very enjoyable way to develop and maintain a good level of fitness. In simple terms, fitness means the overall physical condition of a person, which includes flexibility, speed, strength and endurance. A well-structured karate regime will cover and help develop all four of these elements. Regular training will also help alleviate the stresses of everyday living and lead to an overall better quality of life.

Dojo Etiquette

Good discipline and etiquette within the dojo is of utmost importance. Karate is not all about who can perform the best mawashi geri (roundhouse kick) or who has the strongest punch, but includes the overall attitude and approach to training. This is something Sensei Funakoshi highlighted within his twenty precepts of karate (*see* page 27). The

fifth precept 'Gijutsu yori shinjutsu', when translated, means 'the art of mind is more important than the art of technique'. This is where etiquette and discipline come in. Experience shows that clubs with a high standard of etiquette tend to display a high standard of karate, whereas sloppy etiquette can sometimes permeate into the karate, which in turn becomes sloppy.

Rules of Dojo Etiquette

1. Correct dojo etiquette must be observed at all times.

2. All karateka must bow upon entering and leaving the dojo. The bow must be correctly performed – not just a nod of the head.

3. The dojo is a special place and must be afforded due respect.

4. Correct respect must be shown to the instructor and any visiting sensei.

5. Dan grades should be bowed to in order of seniority prior to commencement of the lesson.

6. Correct respect must be shown to fellow karateka whatever their age or grade. It is customary as a sign of respect to bow to other karateka of a higher grade.

7. Karateka should not arrive or leave in their karate Gi.

8. Good timekeeping is essential. Only in exceptional circumstances will lateness be acceptable. Karateka who arrive late should kneel at the side of the dojo and await invitation from the instructor or sensei to join the class.

9. It is acceptable to stretch and practise

karate techniques in the dojo prior to the commencement of a lesson, provided a class is not in progress. Playing or generally messing around in the dojo is not permitted.

10. When a class is in progress, noise and distraction must be kept to a minimum and due respect afforded.

11. The instructor should be acknowledged regularly during the course of the lesson.

12. Maximum effort, concentration and total commitment to training must be applied at all times.

13. Smoking, eating and drinking is not permitted in the dojo.

14. Karateka should at all times make a personal effort to ensure that their karate Gis are washed and cleaned regularly. Good personal hygiene must be maintained at all times.

15. Toenails and fingernails must be cut short so as to prevent injury to others.

16. Rings, watches, necklaces and other personal adornments must be removed prior to each training session.

17. No abusive or threatening language should be used in the dojo.

18. No unnecessary violence should be used against any person inside or outside of the dojo.

19. Male students should not wear vests or T-shirts under Gis. Female students are permitted to wear a white T-shirt.

Body Language

In any confrontation, whether in the dojo during a competition bout or in a real self-defence situation, body language will play an important part. It can literally be the factor that decides victory or defeat. This is by no means a new philosophy: some 2,500 years ago, the famous Chinese general and military strategist Sun Tzu wrote in *The Art of War* that 'all warfare is based on deception'. So when you feel nervous or weak, think positively and act with assertion. When you are tired, do not show this to your adversary who could be feeling worse. Never give away carelessly your frustrations or true feelings and always try to maintain self-control under pressure. This principle of deception is actually incorporated in a kung fu kata where drunkenness is feigned to lull an attacker into a false sense of security.

4 Fundamental Principles

Karate is a fascinating martial art that has been developed and refined over hundreds of years. It provides a complex system of unarmed combat in which almost every part of the body can be used to good effect. Many of the techniques we use today were developed in feudal times when life or death were the only options. The punching, kicking, striking and blocking techniques had to work and were used to destroy an attacker quickly and decisively.

This historical perspective is important with the advent of karate as a sport because it places modern training practices clearly in context. Unfortunately, many instructors have changed the approach to karate with a shift in emphasis towards training for competitions, neglecting the traditional methods of the past. There are undoubtedly many benefits in competition karate, as this provides the opportunity for offensive and defensive tactics to be used and experimented with under pressure. However, karate should never be considered a sport: it is first and foremost a martial art. The principles outlined in the following chapters are drawn from the more traditional approach, maintaining links with the early development of karate in Japan at the turn of the century.

Proficiency in this art can only be achieved with good instruction and through tireless and repetitive training. This approach is essential if the techniques are to be implanted firmly in the mind so that in times of stress, the blocks, strikes and kicks can be applied automatically, without thinking.

The importance of this automatic, almost reflex response, will be understood by any person who has had the unfortunate experience of having to defend against an unprovoked attack. Under the severe stress associated with being attacked, the body will produce high levels of adrenalin and automatic defensive mechanisms will come into play. The results can be quite staggering. The mind will be incapable of working out complicated defensive or counter-attack strategies, and it is likely that only the major muscle groups will be capable of controlled use. Additionally, peripheral vision may be lost and the ability to hear normally impaired. To help achieve the automatic, reactive response required under these circumstances, a good karateka will spend many hours of incessant and focused training both in the dojo and at home.

However, putting in hours and hours of training will be counter-productive if incorrect technique is being performed. Under these circumstances the only result will be bad habits that prove difficult to get out of. Whether practising blocks, strikes or kicks, concentrate on the detail and be self-critical, avoiding complacency or trying to progress too quickly.

As well as the actual shape or method of delivery of the technique in question, there are a number of fundamental principles that need to be considered at all times.

- Balance and stability
- Factors that affect stability
- The role of the hips
- Relaxation and contraction of the body
- Correct breathing
- Aiming points

Balance and Stability

It goes without saying that good balance and stability are essential if the karate techniques are to be delivered with the speed and power necessary to achieve maximum effect. If this is considered in the context of a punch, it will never realize its full potential if the stance is unstable at the decisive point of impact. Furthermore, with kicking techniques, stability is inherently reduced as soon as the kicking leg is lifted from the ground, so balance and leg control have to be good.

There are four factors that affect balance and stability: the body's mass, the body's centre of gravity, the line of gravity, and the base or stance area. Before considering their effect on balance and stability it is first necessary to understand what is meant by each of these terms.

The Body's Mass

The mass of any object, including the human body, is the amount of matter it contains or the number of particles contained within it. Hence, the bigger the person, the greater the mass.

Centre of Gravity

The centre of gravity of an object is an imaginary point at which the weight of the body acts. This is best explained by an example. Consider a ball – the centre of gravity is located at its geometrical centre. This is the point where half its mass is above and half below, half the mass is located to the left and half to the right, half to the front and half to the back.

This is easy enough to understand when referring to an object such as the ball, but where is the centre of gravity in the human body? The point of the centre of gravity will vary according to the posture and is best described when standing upright in a natural stance. In the diagram (Fig 6), the centre of gravity is located in the centre of the body about 4cm (1½in) below the navel. This point is often referred to by the Japanese as the tanden or hara. The centre of gravity will shift dependent on the activity being undertaken.

Line of Gravity

The line of gravity is simply a line that runs from the centre of gravity down vertically to the ground.

Base Area

The base area encompasses all the parts of the body that are in contact with the

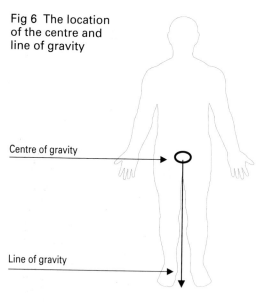

Fig 6 The location of the centre and line of gravity

Centre of gravity

Line of gravity

Fig 7 Heiko dachi

ground at a particular time. In karate this is determined by the stance from which techniques are performed, or in kicking techniques, the foot of the supporting leg. This concept is illustrated using heiko dachi (parallel stance) (Figs 7–9).

Factors that Affect Stability

There are four factors that impact on the body's stability in relation to karate – the body's mass, the height of the centre of gravity, the size of the base or stance area, and the position of the line of gravity.

The Body's Mass

The greater the body's mass or weight, the more stable it will be. Quite clearly it is harder to move someone who is much larger: the

Fig 8 Base area in heiko dachi

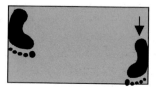

Fig 9 Moving either foot forward or back can increase the size of the base area

downside is, of course, the lack of mobility. A lighter person will be more nimble and able to move more swiftly.

The Height of the Centre of Gravity

The height of the centre of gravity influences the amount of stability. The lower the centre of gravity, the more stable the stance will be. This, however, has to be balanced with the consequential effect on speed of movement, which is proportionately reduced as the centre of gravity is lowered.

The Size of the Base Area

As already mentioned, in karate the base area is determined by the stance from which techniques are performed. This is an important concept to grasp as all of the stances have their own strengths and weaknesses, which in turn will determine when they should, or should not, be used. The bigger the base area, the more stable the position. This can be demonstrated using zenkutsu dachi (front stance) and yoko geri kekomi (side thrust kick) as examples.

In zenkutsu dachi the feet are positioned hip-width apart and the stance is quite long. This provides a large, stable base area (Figs 10–11).

When performing yoko geri kekomi from zenkutsu dachi the resultant reduction in base area is immediately obvious. As soon as the foot is lifted from the ground the base area is substantially reduced to the size of the foot and stability is similarly weakened (Figs 12–13).

It is for this reason that kicks need to be undertaken with speed. The aim should be to

Fig 10 Zenkutsu dachi

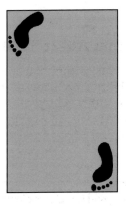

Fig 11 Base area in zenkutsu dachi

35

Fig 12 Yoko geri kekomi

Fig 13 Reduced base area

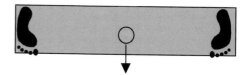

Fig 14 Line of centre of gravity in kiba dachi

deliver the kick as quickly as possible and return the kicking leg to the ground restoring the strong stable position.

The Position of the Line of Gravity

The position of the line of centre of gravity over the base area will affect stability with the most stable position being directly over the centre. The further the line moves from that position, towards and beyond the edge of the base, the greater the instability will be. This is illustrated (Fig 14) using kiba dachi (horse riding stance). As the line moves in the

direction of the arrow the less stable the stance becomes. It will therefore be easy to unbalance someone in kiba dachi by pulling them in the direction of the arrow or pushing in the opposite direction. The stance is stronger to the sides.

The benefits of understanding the underlying principles of balance will now be quite clear. These four factors should be taken into consideration in training and are important aspects to consider when selecting a stance from which to deliver an attack or, alternatively, when considering how best to attack or off-balance an opponent.

The Role of the Hips

Most karate techniques have been designed to take the quickest route to the target. They follow a linear movement and therefore cut out unnecessary body action. This is fairly easy to understand in respect of techniques such as oi zuki (straight punch) or mae geri (front kick), but the principle is often neglected when it comes to the movement of the hips.

Understanding the role of the hips is of utmost importance to the correct performance of karate techniques as they have a primary role to play in almost every move. Whether stepping forward, back or to the sides, or executing a punch, strike, kick or block, it is the hips and stomach muscles that often generate the movement

When moving forward and back or to the sides, keep the hips level at all times, thereby ensuring they, and the centre of gravity, travel through the same plane throughout, in a smooth, flowing movement. This will ensure the quickest route from A to B is taken. Let the hips generate the movement of the legs rather than the other way around.

This principle can be explained more easily by making reference to an example. The photographs (Figs 15–17) illustrate the movement involved in performing an oi zuki while stepping forward in zenkutsu dachi (front stance). The unbroken line indicates the correct movement of the hips, which maintain the same level throughout the movement, and therefore travel in a straight line towards the target. In reality, what often

happens is that the hips are allowed to rise as the feet are drawn together following the route illustrated by the broken line. This results in a slower and weaker movement.

In addition to maintaining the hips and centre of gravity at a constant level, many techniques require the hips to rotate. This helps to ensure that the whole body is used, rather than reliance being placed on the arms or legs alone. Correct use of the hips helps to generate and co-ordinate the movement of the muscles required for the technique resulting in maximization of power.

A good way of practising the hip rotation is to commence in a left zenkutsu dachi, placing the hands on the hips. Start with the hips pulled back so they are positioned sideways-on. From this position, rotate the right hip forward so that it becomes square to the front. Throughout this movement keep the front knee static and the rear foot firmly placed on the floor. The next step is to return the hip back to the start position and repeat.

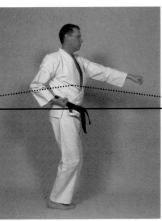

Fig 15   Fig 16   Fig 17

Fig 18 Hips sideways on

Fig 19 Hips square

Ensure that the hips remain level throughout the rotation (Figs 18–19).

Relaxation and Contraction of the Body

Relaxation of the body is essential to maximize speed of movement and is one area that is often misunderstood. If the body is too tense, this will hinder the flow of the movement and speed. To maximize the power of a technique, as much speed as possible needs to be generated over the range of movements. The body should then be tensed for a split second at the very end of the technique or point of impact. This will ensure that the full power of the body is focused at that point. This process is referred to as applying kime (focus) and is the secret to the dynamic and explosive power generated by adept karate exponents. Karate without kime will be severely lacking and it is therefore a concept that must be understood and mastered. Be careful not to tense too soon as de-acceleration will commence at that point.

This feeling of tensing the whole body can be practised while standing in a freestyle stance (Fig 20). From here practise tensing the whole body including the legs, buttocks, stomach, back, chest and arms. Hold the tension for a second, then relax. Tense again for a second and then relax. This should be continued for at least two minutes at a time. It is this tensing of the whole body that should take place at the end of each strike, block or kick.

In attacking moves the power can be increased by locking the rear leg and pushing back into the floor to coincide with the tensing of the body. This should create a reactionary force moving forward.

Do not over exert on the blocking techniques unless the block is used as an attacking move. Only use as much force as is necessary

Fig 20 Freestyle stance

and then reply by delivering an explosive counter-attack with full kime. The faster the muscle is tensed, provided the timing is correct, the more power in the technique.

Correct Breathing

Breathing is something that is done automatically and often taken for granted. Nonetheless, it is useful to understand the mechanics of breathing and what actually takes place within the body with each breath. The importance of correct breathing in karate will then become self-evident.

The body requires a constant supply of oxygen in order that the cells can break down the food we eat to produce energy. On inhalation the lungs fill up with air and oxygen is absorbed into the blood. The blood is then carried to the heart from where it is pumped around the body in the red blood cells and used in the metabolic process to produce the energy. On exhalation the waste carbon dioxide is removed from the blood via the lungs.

Most people breathe only superficially using about 6 per cent of the capacity of the lungs, starving the body of oxygen and preventing the complete exhalation of the carbon dioxide. Inhalation should be via the nose, which will warm, and clean the incoming air. Exhalation should be through the mouth on execution of the karate techniques. Maximize the use of the diaphragm so that breathing is not short and shallow. Well-regulated breathing will help the body to relax and strong exhalation will enhance the kime at point of impact.

When practising with a partner, maintain

good breath control and try not to show signs of fatigue. Concentrate on the breathing of your partner and, where possible, attack when breath is being inhaled, thus providing a competitive advantage. It is harder to tense and move when breathing in.

Aiming Points

The subject of vulnerable and vital points is covered in more detail in Chapter 10. However, this is an important area and merits mention here. Always try to visualize the purpose of the movement being undertaken and concentrate on aiming points that will be realistic and effective. Only use as much power as is necessary.

Karate is a martial art designed to destroy the body of an attacker. Whether it be disruption of the nervous, respiratory, or circulatory systems, breaking of joints or gouging of body parts, the techniques must work. Remember there may only be one chance. When performing kata, the aiming points and the purpose of the moves being undertaken must be understood and considered at all times if the form is to have meaning and full benefit derived.

When training with a partner during kumite, always concentrate on directing the counter-attacks to areas of your partner's body where maximum effect will be achieved. In time this approach will train the mind to respond in this way automatically.

5 Dachi (Stances) Theory and Practice

Although the importance of stance training can never be overstated, it is an area that is often neglected. Regularly, students in the dojo can be seen tirelessly practising their delivery of kicks, or going through complicated kumite routines, but rarely will any emphasis be placed on stance development.

Consider a stance like the foundations of a building. If the foundations are weak, the building will topple and fall. If good and strong, the building will stand for eternity. A strong stance will provide the stability that is paramount to the effective delivery of karate techniques. A punch, for instance, will never realize its full potential if executed from a poor and weak base.

When selecting a stance, the role of the body's centre of gravity, covered in detail within Chapter 4, must be understood. The lower the centre of gravity, the stronger stability will be. However, having said this, a compromise must be reached. As the centre of gravity is lowered, speed of movement becomes more and more restricted. In effect, someone positioned in a very low zenkutsu dachi (front stance) may be virtually immovable but will be unable to generate great speed between techniques. Conversely, a

high stance will be weak but will allow greater speed of movement. With this in mind, the karate stances were developed to optimize both strength and speed of movement and therefore must be understood and applied correctly.

At first, many of the stances will feel unnatural and uncomfortable until the joints and muscles become accustomed to the position. One method of training is to get into a correct stance and then hold the position until the muscles ache. Maintain this position for as long as possible. When it becomes too much, change so that the opposite leg becomes the leading leg and repeat the process. For extra benefit, try tensing all the muscles in the legs, buttocks, stomach and back simultaneously and hold the tension for ten seconds. Repeat up to ten times in each stance. It may feel uncomfortable but this method of training will pay dividends in the long run.

Perfecting each stance and developing the ability to move freely and effectively from one to another will take many years of repetitive training. Nevertheless, this should be one of the ultimate goals. The hips also have a vital role to play in this. When moving between stances, use the hips and stomach muscles to generate the movement and try to ensure that the hips move smoothly along the same plane throughout. The feet should glide across the floor so that both feet remain in contact with the floor at all times. A common error is to step or jump between stances.

Generally speaking, there are fifteen different stances that are utilized in traditional karate styles.

- Heisoku dachi (informal attention stance)
- Musubi dachi (informal attention stance)
- Heiko dachi (parallel stance)
- Hachiji dachi (open leg stance)
- Teiji dachi (T-stance)
- Renoji dachi (L-stance)
- Zenkutsu dachi (front stance)
- Kokutsu dachi (back stance)
- Kiba dachi (horse riding or straddle leg stance)
- Shiko dachi (square stance)
- Fudo dachi (rooted stance)
- Neko ashi dachi (cat stance)
- Hengetsu dachi (half-moon stance)
- Sanchin dachi (hour-glass stance)
- Kosa dachi (cross-legged stance)

Six of the stances (heisoku dachi, musubi dachi, hachiji dachi, heiko dachi, teiji dachi and renoji dachi) are relatively easy to learn. The remainder are much more complex in nature, each providing its own unique difficulties.

A truly adept karate exponent will, through years of training, develop the ability to move freely from one stance to another without thinking, each time arriving in the correct form with the correct weight distribution. This in turn will provide the base and stability from which the powerful karate techniques can be delivered with full effect.

Heisoku Dachi and Musubi Dachi (Informal Attention Stances)

Heisoku dachi and musubi dachi are usually the first stances to be taught and are often utilized when performing the rei (bow) (Figs 2–24).

Heisoku dachi is also used regularly during the performance of kata or as an intermediate stance during the transition from one move to another. When performing heisoku dachi the feet are placed together. In musubi dachi, although the heels meet, the feet are turned out at an angle of 45 degrees. In both cases, the body's weight should be evenly distributed between the two feet.

Common Mistakes
In both heisoku dachi and musubi dachi, the two most common mistakes are failure to keep the heels of the feet touching, and locking the legs straight. Bend the knees slightly and remain relaxed. In heisoku dachi there is often a tendency to allow the feet to turn out. Concentrate on keeping the feet parallel.

Rei (Bow)
One of the first moves taught in traditional karate styles is the bow. Heisoku dachi is the stance used in this instance, but some associations use musubi dachi.

Fig 21 Heisoku dachi

Fig 23 Musubi dachi

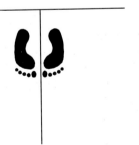

Fig 22 Heisoku dachi foot placement

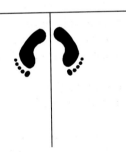

Fig 24 Musubi dachi foot placement

Fig 25 Front view

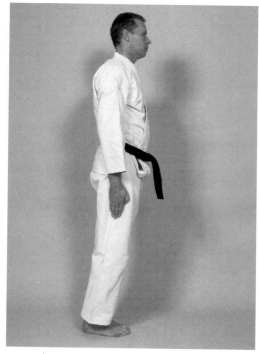

Fig 26 Side view

Assume heisoku dachi with the hands lightly touching the sides of the legs and the palms turned inward. Stand tall with the back straight. When performing the bow, bend at the waist keeping the hands unchanged at the side of the legs (Figs 25–27).

The Japanese consider excessive eye contact to be impolite and this should be avoided when bowing to a partner. The depth of the bow varies according to the importance of the person to whom the bow is being directed. The more important the person, the deeper the bow. In karate the bow should be to about 30 degrees.

Common Mistakes

There are a number of common mistakes associated with the bow. In particular the position of the hands needs to be watched. The hands are often incorrectly placed either at the back, clutching the buttocks, or positioned to the front, against the thighs. When the hands are placed correctly at the sides ensure that the fingers are closed and not splayed apart.

Fig 27 The bow

Fig 28 Heiko dachi

Heiko Dachi (Parallel Stance) and Hachiji Dachi (Open Leg Stance)

Heiko dachi and hachiji dachi are very similar and both involve moving the feet out to the side. In both of these stances the feet should be just over hip-width apart with the knees slightly bent. The weight distribution should be evenly balanced. In hachiji dachi the feet are turned out sideways at an angle of 45 degrees, while in heiko dachi they remain pointed forward and parallel. In both stances,

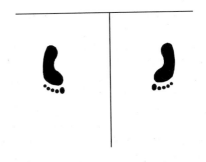

Fig 29 Heiko dachi foot placement

45

Fig 30 Hachiji dachi

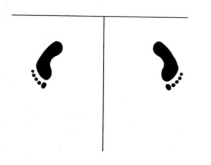

Fig 31 Hachiji dachi foot placement

keep the body relaxed while remaining alert and aware. A relaxed body is capable of faster and greater fluidity of movement (Figs 28–31).

Yoi (Ready Position)

Following the bow it is customary to step out into the yoi position. It is from here that all other techniques are performed (Figs 32–35).

STEP 1

Assume the heisoku dachi position with the hands at the side as if just having completed the bow.

STEP 2

Step out with the right foot so that the feet become just over hip-width apart in heiko dachi. At the same time cross the hands in front of the body with the right hand on top.

STEP 3

Pull both hands back to the hips as fists with the palm of the hand facing upward.

STEP 4

Push forward with both hands while keeping them clenched. The fists should complete the move level with the hips and turned in at an angle of 45 degrees. On completion of the movement both the arms and the knees should be slightly bent and the body relaxed.

When stepping out into the yoi position it is important to breathe in through the nose during Steps 1–3 and out through the mouth as the hands are pushed forward in Step 4.

46

Fig 32 Step 1

Fig 33 Step 2

Fig 34 Step 3

Fig 35 Step 4

Common Mistakes

While in the yoi position the body should be totally relaxed. One of the more common mistakes is to remain too tense and rigid throughout this move. Concentrate on keeping the legs and arms slightly bent to aid relaxation.

There are often variations in the positioning of the hands at the completion of the move. The hands must remain as fists but not tightly clenched. Their position should be turned in slightly. It should be noted that some associations employ a variation of these arm movements although the other considerations remain consistent (Fig 36).

Teiji Dachi (T-Stance) and Renoji Dachi (L-Stance)

Teiji dachi and renoji dachi are similar in nature. In both cases the feet should remain flat on the floor and the weight distribution even. Both stances are utilized in kata and in the transition from stance to stance.

In teiji dachi, as the name implies, the feet are positioned so as to form a letter 'T'. The heel of the front foot should be in line with the centre of the rear foot with a distance between the feet of about 30cm (12in) (Figs 37–38).

Fig 36 Correct hand positioning

Fig 37 Teiji dachi

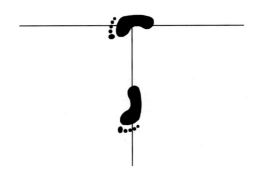

Fig 38 Teiji dachi foot placement

In renoji dachi, again as the name implies, the feet are positioned so as to form a letter 'L', the heel of the front foot being placed in line with the heel of the rear foot, thereby forming the 'L' shape. As with teiji dachi, the distance between the feet should be about 30cm (12in) (Figs 39–40).

Common Mistakes
A common mistake with both teiji dachi and renoji dachi is weight distribution. There is a tendency to shift the weight either backward or forward in preparation for the next technique. Keep the weight evenly distributed and both feet placed firmly on the floor.

Zenkutsu Dachi (Front Stance)

This is perhaps the most widely used stance in karate and is therefore covered in detail. If performed correctly it provides great strength and stability in both defence and attack.

Fig 39 Renoji dachi

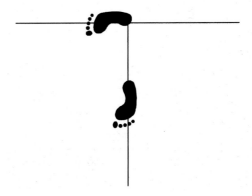

Fig 40 Renoji dachi foot placement

To perform the stance correctly, the feet should be positioned so that they are hip-width apart with both feet remaining flat on the floor. The front foot should be pointing forward and the rear foot at an angle of at least 45 degrees. The front knee needs be bent far enough forward so that the shin-bone is perpendicular to the ground and the rear leg should be locked straight on completion of the stance. The body must also remain upright with the weight distribution being 60 per cent over the front foot and the remaining 40 per cent over the rear foot (Figs 41–43).

Fig 42 Front view

Fig 41 Side view

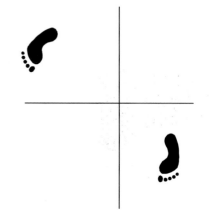

Fig 43 Zenkutsu dachi foot placement

Common Mistakes

There are a number of common mistakes associated with zenkutsu dachi that are worthy of consideration. Often the stance is too short. This is understandable in the early months of training because the body is being asked to get into a position that is quite unnatural at first. Getting accustomed to stepping in a long stance will take time but every effort should be made to achieve this.

In a correct zenkutsu dachi the feet should be positioned hip-width apart with both feet flat on the floor. Frequently this stance is completed with the feet in line, which makes it unstable. This can also result in the rear foot rising off the floor either on to the ball of the foot or the inside edge of the foot.

The following photographs illustrate a number of other problem areas associated with this stance.

The rear foot is turned out to the rear, which is incorrect. Concentrate on turning the rear foot towards the front as far as possible and in any case at an angle of at least 45 degrees (Fig 44).

The front foot is turned out to the side, which is incorrect. Concentrate on keeping the foot pointing forward (Fig 45).

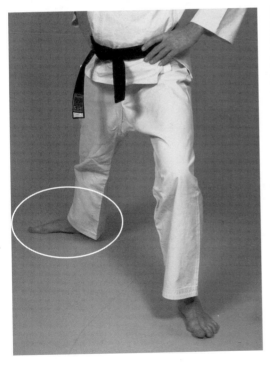

Fig 44 Incorrect rear foot position.

Fig 45 Incorrect front foot position.

Fig 46 Incorrect – leaning back

Throughout the stance keep the back upright. Concentrate on leaning neither to the rear nor to the front (Figs 46–47).

The front knee has caved in, which is incorrect. Concentrate on keeping the knee upright on completion of the stance (Fig 48).

Stepping Forward and Back
Stepping forward and back in zenkutsu dachi appears relatively easy to do at first sight. However, there are a number of considerations to take into account. At all times keep the back upright and use the hips and

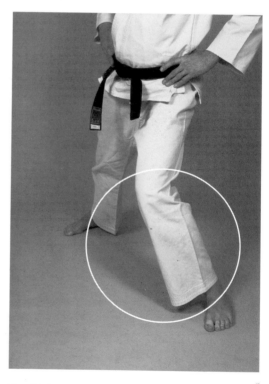

Fig 48 Incorrect – front knee turned inward

Fig 47 Incorrect – leaning forward

stomach muscles to drive the body forward. Throughout the movement the hips must remain at the same height, avoiding the tendency to rise as the feet are brought together only to drop back down on stepping through (Figs 49–51).

STEP 1
Start in zenkutsu dachi with the left foot forward. Ensure that the feet are positioned hip-width apart and the back upright.

STEP 2
Move the rear foot up to centre so that it inscribes an arc and is drawn level with and touching the front foot. Keep the knees bent so that the hips do not rise at this point, and keep the back straight.

STEP 3
Continue stepping through by sliding the right foot forward in a circular movement so that a long zenkutsu dachi is made with the feet finishing hip-width apart. The rear leg should lock straight at the end of the movement.

To step backward, simply reverse the action described above by pulling the front foot back to the centre and then out to the rear in a circular movement so the feet again end hip-width apart in a long zenkutsu dachi.

Fig 49 Step 1

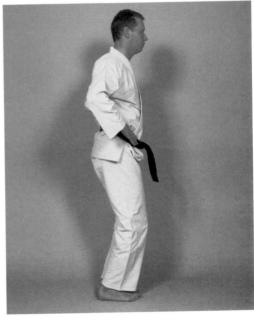

Fig 50 Step 2

Fig 51 Step 3

Common Mistakes
As well as the general mistakes already covered above in respect of zenkutsu dachi there are some other common errors to watch for when stepping forward or back in this stance. The most common error is the failure to inscribe the circular action with the foot and complete the stance with the feet hip-width apart. What often happens is that the feet step through in a straight line, resulting in instability.

When stepping backward, concentrate on keeping the back upright, as it is a common mistake to lean forward in the first instance in order to generate the momentum to pull the leading leg back. Use the hips and stomach muscles to create the movement.

Turning

Turning often causes a lot of problems for people first starting out in karate. In fact, the actual process is not that complicated when broken down: it is a case of getting the mind around the movements concerned.

The turn in zenkutsu dachi will be broken down into three parts. In the first stage only the leg movements will be covered, in the second stage the turn will include a gedan bari (downward block), and in the third stage the turn used in kata will be explained. It is advisable only to move on to the second and third stages once the first can be achieved satisfactorily.

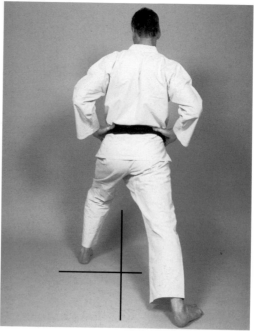

Fig 52 Step 1

Stage 1 (Figs 52–54)
STEP 1
Start off in a left zenkutsu dachi with the feet hip-width apart.

STEP 2
Look over the right shoulder. Step across in a straight line with the rear (right) foot so that the foot moves level with the front foot and then the same distance again beyond.

STEP 3
At this point imagine that someone has driven a nail through both feet. The feet can

pivot on the spot but not move in any other way. While pivoting on the feet, rotate the hips to face the opposite direction and complete the turn. Simultaneously, transfer the weight over to the right (now front) foot.

Common Mistakes
The most common mistake with this turn is failure to move the back leg far enough across before rotating the hips. More often than not, the rear leg is moved only so far as to be positioned level with the front foot. As a result, when the turn is complete, the body is

Fig 53 Step 2

Fig 54 Step 3

not facing in the correct direction and the stance becomes unstable.

Stage 2

Having mastered the turning action with the feet the next stage is to use the arms to simultaneously block with a gedan barai (Figs 55–57). (*See also* Chapter 7 where gedan barai is covered in more detail.)

STEP 1

Commence in a gedan barai position in left zenkutsu dachi. Again make sure that the feet are hip-width apart.

STEP 2

Look over the right shoulder and step across in a straight line with the rear (right) foot. At the same time move the right hand to the left neck position and push the left hand around in the direction of the turn.

STEP 3

Pivoting on the feet, rotate the hips to face the opposite direction. With the right hand perform a gedan barai and withdraw the left hand to the hip to complete the turn.

Common Mistakes

In addition to the mistakes in turning already described, the main problem that arises when adding the gedan barai is failure to use both arms in the blocking action as described in

Fig 55 Step 1

Fig 56 Step 2

become easier. A gedan barai is also included in the following example (Figs 58–61).

STEP 1
Commence in a gedan barai position in left zenkutsu dachi.

STEP 2
Look over the left shoulder and simultaneously pull the front (left) foot back to meet the right foot. At the same time move the left hand to the left neck position and push the right hand around towards the direction of the turn.

Fig 57 Step 3

Fig 58 Step 1

Step 2 above. Often the block is performed using one-handed techniques with the blocking arm only, reducing the overall power that can be applied.

Stage 3
The third aspect of turning in zenkutsu dachi is that used in kata. Kata are training exercises involving a variety of pre-determined moves against imaginary opponents and form an important part of traditional karate training. Once this third aspect of turning is understood, the grasp of early kata will

Fig 59 Step 2

Fig 60 Step 3

STEP 3

Continue to step through with the left foot diagonally to the left. The hands remain unchanged at this stage.

STEP 4

Pivoting on the feet, rotate the hips to face the opposite direction. With the left hand, perform a gedan barai and withdraw the right hand to the hip to complete the turn.

Common Mistakes

The most common mistake with this turn is in relation to the movement of the foot between Steps 1 and 3. It is important that the foot travels diagonally across and not back in a straight line, which is how the move is often incorrectly performed (Fig 62).

Kokutsu Dachi (Back Stance)

This is a widely practised stance but one of the hardest to perform correctly. During the early months of training, this stance will feel very unnatural and awkward. A great deal of perseverance is required if improvements are to be made.

When performed correctly the heels of the feet should be in line, with the front foot pointing forward and the rear foot sideways so that a right angle is formed. The front knee should be slightly bent to relieve the pressure on the knee, and hips positioned sideways-on. There should be a feeling of sitting over the rear leg so that the weight distribution is 70 per cent over the rear and the remaining 30 per cent over the front leg (Figs 63–64).

Common Mistakes
There are a number of common mistakes associated with kokutsu dachi that are worthy of consideration. Because the stance is quite unnatural, the tendency is for it to be too short. The length of the stance should be the same as zenkutsu dachi and movement between the two can be achieved by shifting the weight and centre of gravity without shortening the length between the feet.

Fig 61 Step 4

The front knee should be slightly bent – a common mistake is to perform the stance

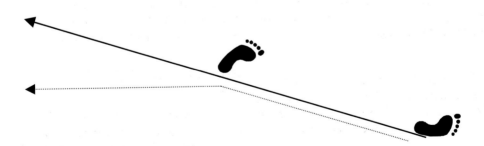

Fig 62 Correct and incorrect foot movement in turning. The dotted line illustrates the incorrect line of travel whereas the solid line indicates the route through which the foot should travel

Fig 63 Kokutsu dachi

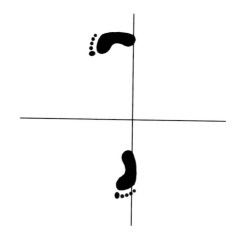

Fig 64 Kokutsu dachi foot placement

Fig 65 Incorrect – knee should not be locked straight

with the front knee locked straight (Fig 65).

The rear foot should point to the side and the front foot forward. It is not uncommon for either the rear foot to be turned out at a greater angle to the side or for the front foot to be turned in. Both are incorrect (Figs 66–67).

Do not allow the rear knee to cave in on completion of the stance. Concentrate on forcing the knee backward and keeping the backside tucked in (Fig 68).

Fig 66 Incorrect –
rear foot turned out

Fig 67 Incorrect – front
foot turned in

Fig 68 Incorrect – rear
knee caving in

Stepping Forward and Back

The process of stepping forward and back in kokutsu dachi is similar to that of zenkutsu dachi (front stance). The main variation is that in this instance the feet do not make the circular movements of zenkutsu dachi but travel through in a straight line (Figs 69–71).

STEP 1
Start in kokutsu dachi with the left foot forward. Ensure that the heels are in line and the body positioned sideways-on.

STEP 2
Move the rear foot up to centre in a straight line until it is drawn level with and touching

Fig 69 Step 1

Fig 70 Step 2

Fig 71 Step 3

the front foot. Keep the knees bent so that the hips do not rise at this point, and keep the back straight.

STEP 3

Continue stepping through by sliding the right foot forward in a straight line so that a long kokutsu dachi is made with the feet finishing with the heels in line. The rear leg should be bent and pushed back .

Remember to keep the back upright at all times and use the hips and stomach muscles to propel the body forward. Keep the hips at the same height throughout the movement.

To step backward, simply reverse the action described above. Pull the front foot back to the centre and then out to the rear in a straight line so the heels are aligned in a long kokutsu dachi.

Common Mistakes

As well as the general mistakes already covered in respect of kokutsu dachi, there are some other common problems associated with stepping forward or back in this stance.

The most common mistake is failure to step through long enough and in a straight line. Frequently, the feet end up quite wide, which makes it difficult to distinguish between this stance and zenkutsu dachi.

When stepping forward and back, concentrate on keeping the back upright – it is a common mistake to lean forward with the backside sticking out.

Turning
The turning action in kokutsu dachi is not dissimilar to zenkutsu dachi (Figs 72–74).

STEP 1
Start in the shuto uke (knife hand block) position in kokutsu dachi with the right foot forward and ensure that the feet are positioned with the heels in line.

STEP 2
Look over the left shoulder and move the left hand to the right shoulder. At the same time

Fig 73 Step 2

push the right hand in the direction of the turn.

STEP 3
Pivoting on the feet, rotate the hips to face the opposite direction and complete the turn. Simultaneously, block with a left shuto uke. When the turn is complete, 70 per cent of the body's weight should be transferred to the rear leg.

Common Mistakes
The most common mistakes in this turn involve the hand position both in the intermediate position at the neck, and on

Fig 72 Step 1

63

Fig 74 Step 3

Kiba Dachi (Horse Riding or Straddle Leg Stance)

This is a strong stance for delivery of attacks to the side such as yoko empi (elbow strike to the side) or yoko geri kekomi (side thrust kick).

In kiba dachi both feet should be pointing forward and parallel, with the weight evenly distributed between the two. The feet should be about twice hip-width apart and the knees pushed outward. The body must be upright with the hips pushed forward (Figs 75–76).

completion of the block. At the halfway stage, check the hand position to ensure the palm of the hand is facing in towards the neck. On completion of the block there should be a right angle at the inside of the elbow.

There is also a tendency to lean backward too much at the end of the technique. Remember to keep the back upright at all times, and the palm of the blocking hand facing out.

Fig 75 Kiba dachi

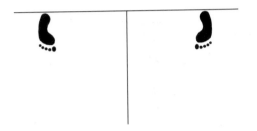

Fig 76 Kiba dachi foot placement

Common Mistakes
Many of the common mistakes are a consequence of stiffness in the hip joints and can be overcome with perseverance.

Do not allow the knees to cave inward (Fig 77). Concentrating on forcing the knees out so they are almost positioned above the feet can make an improvement. Once this is achieved, drop the weight down and push the hips forward. Ensure that the back is kept upright throughout.

Other mistakes associated with kiba dachi concern the position of the feet, which are often allowed to turn out to the side instead of remaining parallel; and the stance, which is often too short (Fig 78).

Fig 77 Incorrect – knees turned in

Fig 78 Incorrect – feet turned out and legs too straight

Stepping Forward and Back

The process of stepping in kiba dachi is fairly straightforward and easy to get to grips with (Figs 79–81).

STEP 1
Commence in a kiba dachi stance, looking over the left shoulder. Pull the hands backward so that the shoulder blades are squeezed together and the back is upright.

STEP 2
Keep looking to the left and do not move the arms. Step with the right foot across the front of the left shin to a halfway stage. The hips should retain the same height.

Fig 80 Step 2

Fig 79 Step 1

STEP 3
Continuing to look to the left and without moving the arms, step out with the left foot back into a kiba dachi to complete the move.

The turn in kiba dachi is simply a sharp turn of the head to face the opposite direction. It is then possible to step back as described below.

STEP 4
Having turned to the right, keep looking in that direction and do not move the arms. Step with the left foot across the front of the right shin to a halfway stage.

Fig 81 Step 3

Step 5

Continuing to look to the right and without moving the arms, step out with the right foot back into a kiba dachi to complete the move.

Common Mistakes

The important point to remember when stepping in kiba dachi is that the feet must follow a course to ensure that the movement in the stance is in a straight line. As well as the common mistakes already described, this is another area where the stance can cause problems (Fig 82).

Shiko Dachi (Square Stance)

Shiko dachi is similar to kiba dachi (horse riding or straddle leg stance) except the feet are turned outward at an angle of 45 degrees. Again the body must be upright with the feet about twice hip-width apart and the knees pushed out (Figs 83–84).

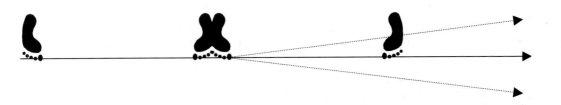

Fig 82 The correct positioning of the feet at the start and completion of the move is shown on the unbroken line whereas the dotted lines show the incorrect routes that are often taken

67

Fig 83 Shiko dachi

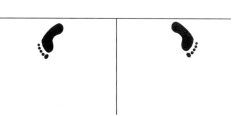

Fig 84 Shiko dachi foot placement

are positioned hip-width apart and pointed sideways at an angle of about 45 degrees. The knees of both legs should be bent (Figs 85–86).

Jiyu Kumite Gamae (Freestyle Stance)

The type of stance used for freestyle kumite is ultimately down to personal choice and there are many variations to be found. Fudo dachi is a good freestyle stance because it is

Fig 85 Fudo dachi

Fudo Dachi (Rooted Stance)

Fudo dachi is a stance halfway between zenkutsu dachi (front stance) and kiba dachi. The weight distribution is slightly forward with 55 per cent over the front leg and the remaining 45 per cent over the rear. The feet

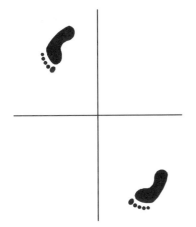

Fig 86 Fudo dachi foot placement

both strong and agile, offering a good compromise between speed and stability (Fig 87).

Neko Ashi Dachi (Cat Stance)

Neko ashi dachi, as the name implies, is a very light stance that enables speed of movement. The weight should be distributed so that 90 per cent is over the rear leg and only 10 per cent over the front. The rear foot should be pointed sideways at an angle of 45 degrees, and the front foot pointed forward

Fig 87 Fudo dachi freestyle stance

Fig 88 Neko ashi dachi

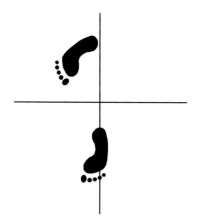

Fig 89 Neko ashi dachi foot placement

Fig 90 Hengetsu dachi

so that the heels of both feet are in line. The distance between the two feet should approximately hip-width. The front foot should be raised so that the ball of the foot makes light contact with the floor (Figs 88–89).

Hengetsu Dachi (Half-Moon Stance)

Hengetsu dachi will feel very awkward and uncomfortable when first learnt, but once mastered is a strong, solid stance and can be used to good effect in both defence and attack.

Both feet should be pointing in the same direction and at a slight angle to the side. Both knees must be bent and pushed inward with the weight evenly distributed between both feet. Concentrate on extending the spine by dropping the weight down at the hips and pushing up with the head. The

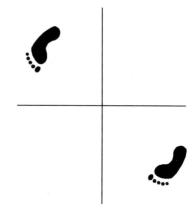

Fig 91 Hengetsu dachi foot placement

stance should be slightly shorter than zenkutsu dachi (front stance) (Figs 90–91).

Sanchin Dachi (Hour-Glass Stance)

There are some similarities between sanchin dachi and hengetsu dachi (half-moon stance). The feet should be hip-width apart with the weight evenly distributed. The rear foot must point forward with the front foot turned in. From this position, bend the knees

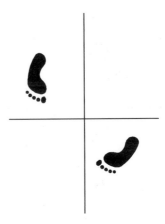

Fig 93 Sanchin dachi foot placement

so that they are over the toes of each foot. This will have the feeling of the knees being pushed inward (Figs 92–93).

Kosa Dachi (Cross-Legged Stance)

Kosa dachi is a stance that often crops up in kata and is included here to provide a reference point and, hopefully, a better understanding of its make up.

Place the right foot on the ground, pointing to the front. Then move the left foot up to the back of the right and on to the ball of the foot. The shin of the left leg should make contact with the calf muscle of the right. Keep the back upright and bend the knees, which will result in the hips dropping (Figs 94–95).

Seiza (Seated Position)

The following series of photographs demonstrates the movement from heisoku dachi

Fig 92 Sanchin dachi

71

Fig 94 Kosa dachi – front view

Fig 95 Kosa dachi – side view

(informal attention stance) into seiza. It is from this stance that mokuso (meditation) is undertaken and the dojo kun is recited (*see* page 27).

The order in which the legs and arms move is important and must be followed carefully. The samurai developed this sequence in ancient times so that the sword could be drawn with minimal hindrance. This explains why, when kneeling, the left knee and hand precede the right. In doing so the sword can always be drawn more easily. Like most moves in karate, nothing is undertaken aimlessly.

In the example that follows, the sequence of moves commences from the heisoku dachi (informal attention stance) position. This does not always have to be the case – musubi dachi is also used (Figs 96–99).

STEP 1
Commence in heisoku dachi, hands lightly touching the sides of the legs.

STEP 2
From heisoku dachi squat down on the balls of the feet and kneel down, left knee first followed by the right.

Fig 96 Step 1

Fig 97 Step 2 (a)

Fig 98 Step 2 (b)

Fig 99 Step 2 (c)

From the seiza position the dojo kun can then be recited. It is traditional for the senior grade present to call out the dojo kun, each line in turn, which is then repeated by the remainder of the class. At the end of the recitation, the senior student will then call out the command 'shomen ni rei' which means 'bow to the front'. The bow should then made to the front following the steps described below (Figs 100–102).

STEP 1
From the seiza position, place the left hand on the floor first.

STEP 2
Place the right hand on the floor and bow to the front. At this point the eyes should remain

Fig 101 Step 2 (a)

Fig 100 Step 1

Fig 102 Step 2 (b)

open and the mind alert. The head should be positioned so that any movement from the rear can be picked up early.

STEP 3

To return to seiza position, the process described above is merely reversed.

At this point it is traditional to perform a further bow to the sensei on the command 'sensei ni rei'. The bow should follow the steps described above.

Each of the steps described above should then be reversed on command to return to the standing position in heisoku dachi.

6 Uchi (Striking) Theory and Practice

As karate has evolved over the years, a variety of zuki (punching) and uchi (striking) techniques have been developed and fine-tuned so that almost every part of the hand or arm can be used to good effect. This enables decisive attacking techniques to be delivered in any direction with both speed and power.

This chapter covers the more frequently used punches and strikes. These must not be viewed in isolation – the blocking techniques covered in the next chapter can also serve as equally effective strikes in given circumstances. Also, it is important to understand that a strike may be made with many parts of the body, provided it is realistic and works.

Movements using the hands and arms are generally more effective at close range, being faster and more versatile than their kicking counterparts. The disadvantage is that they are not as powerful as kicks, and greater consideration is needed in selection of the target area. However, the versatility of the arms and hands enables the strikes to be targeted at parts of the body not readily accessible by kicking techniques. This becomes more an issue in the study of kyusho (pressure point) striking.

The correct application of a punch or strike will not rely solely on the strength and/or speed of the arm being used. Other issues should be borne in mind such as distancing, kime (focus), and the aiming points of the body. Correct use of stances and the hips will also assist in ensuring optimum power is realized at the point of delivery of the technique. These issues should be taken into consideration at all times during training.

When punching, the weak part of the arm is the wrist, which can buckle on impact, weakening the technique and causing injury. In severe cases, the resultant injury can incapacitate the arm, rendering it virtually useless. For this reason, open-handed techniques such as teisho (palm heel strike) or shuto (knife hand strike) are often considered to be more appropriate.

In this chapter the punches and strikes are demonstrated on one side of the body only. In practice, both sides must be used so that the techniques are equally effective, regardless of the side from which they are delivered. They should also be practised stepping forward and back and at different angles, the intention being to develop the ability to deliver an attack to any direction.

The principal techniques covered in this chapter are:

- Choku zuki (straight punch)
- Oi zuki (stepping punch)
- Gyaku zuki (reverse punch)
- Tate zuki (vertical punch)
- Age zuki (rising punch)
- Ura zuki (close punch)
- Kizami zuki (jabbing punch)
- Shuto uchi (knife hand strike)
- Haito uchi (ridge hand strike)
- Uraken uchi (back fist strike)
- Teisho uchi (palm heel strike)
- Hiraken uchi (fore knuckle strike)
- Nukite uchi (spear hand strike)
- Ippon ken uchi (one knuckle strike)
- Nakadaka ken uchi (middle finger strike)
- Tetsui uchi (bottom fist strike)
- Nihon nukite (two finger strike)
- Empi uchi (elbow strike).

Making a Fist

Correct formation of the fist is important in all punching techniques. This may seem very basic, but small mistakes are often made and it is a useful exercise to start from this point (Figs 103–105).

STEP 1

Commence by raising both hands above the head. Keep the hands open with the palms facing forward.

STEP 2

The next step is to roll the fingers of both hands down, keeping the thumbs pointing out.

STEP 3

Complete the fists by clenching the fingers and tucking the thumbs in across the knuckles.

Fig 103 Step 1   Fig 104 Step 2   Fig 105 Step 3

It is at this point that problems start to occur. Common mistakes include tucking the thumbs in behind the index finger or pressing them against the outer edge of the index finger. The completed fist should end with the fingers clenched and the thumb tucked in across the fingers (Fig 106).

Choku Zuki (Straight Punch)

Choku zuki is the most basic karate punch and is usually the first one to be taught. It is normally performed in heiko dachi (parallel stance) to enable concentration to be focused on the arm movements without the need to worry about the more complicated positioning of the feet (Figs 107–112).

Commence by assuming the yoi (ready) position in heiko dachi.

Fig 107 Yoi position

STEP 1
From the yoi position, bring both arms up in front of the body, keeping the fists clenched with the back of the hands facing upward.

STEP 2
Turning the hand 180 degrees, bring the right fist back to the right hip, keeping the left hand in position.

STEP 3
Punch by driving the right hand forward and rotating the hand 180 degrees, while simultaneously pulling the left hand back to the hip.

STEP 4
Repeat on the opposite side by punching with the left fist, while simultaneously pulling the right fist back to the right hip.

Fig 106 Correct formation of a fist

78

Fig 108 Step 1

Fig 109 Step 2

Fig 110 Step 3 (a)

Fig 111 Step 3 (b)

Fig 112 Step 3 (c)

On a more technical note, the smaller the striking surface (or mass) of the hand, the less resistance it will meet on impact, which will result in greater penetration (Fig 113).

This punch should be practised continuously, aiming at different levels as confidence increases.

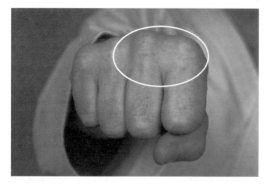

Fig 113 The striking point of the fist is the two fore knuckles

Common Mistakes

There are a number of faults frequently made when performing this punch. These also apply to the other punching techniques covered in this chapter. When punching within the dojo this technique should be practised with the solar plexus as the aiming point. This means that the punch will need to be directed at a slightly downward angle and to the centre of the body.

Often the punch is directed too wide or high (Fig 114).

The shoulders need to be kept square throughout the punch. A common mistake is to lead in with the shoulder of the punching arm (Fig 115).

Remember to keep the back upright so that the spine is straight and just use the arms at

Fig 114 Incorrect – punch too wide

Fig 115 Incorrect – right shoulder leading

Fig 117 Incorrect – hand dropped

Fig 116 Incorrect – hand turned in

this stage, making sure that the shoulders remain square.

At the completion of the technique, the hand of the non-punching arm should be drawn back to the hip.

Check that the fist is positioned so that the palm is facing upward and the elbow is tucked in. It is common for the fist to end up hanging down or turned palm-inward at this stage (Figs 116–117).

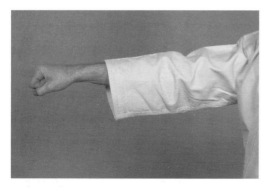

Fig 118 Correct punching technique

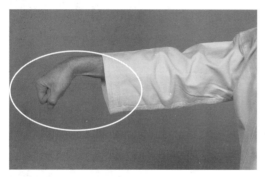

Fig 119 Incorrect – wrist bent down

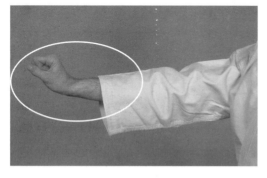

Fig 120 Incorrect – wrist bent up

The wrist must be kept straight at all times. Do not let it bend up or down as this will result in poor technique and could cause wrist damage on impact (Figs 118–120).

Oi Zuki (Stepping Punch)

This basic karate punch is performed while moving. It is usually practised stepping forward and back in zenkutsu dachi (front stance), which is how it is demonstrated in the example below (Figs 121–124). The punching action of the arms is the same as that for choku zuki (straight punch) described above.

STEP 1
Assume the left gedan barai (downward block) position in zenkutsu dachi.

STEP 2
Step forward with the right leg so that the feet are positioned together, pushing out with the left hand. The hips should remain square-on to the front and at the same level, avoiding the tendency to raise the hips as the feet come together.

STEP 3
Keeping the hands where they are, step forward half a pace with the right leg.

STEP 4
Continue to step forward with the right leg into a full zenkutsu dachi and punch with the right fist while simultaneously bringing the left hand back to the hip.

As with choku zuki this punch should then be practised on the opposite side.

Fig 121 Step 1

Fig 122 Step 2

Fig 123 Step 3

Fig 124 Step 4

Common Mistakes

Some of the common mistakes made when punching have already been covered in choku zuki. When performing oi zuki, concentration must be focused on delivering the punch in a good stance. This punch is normally practised in zenkutsu dachi, and often the punching technique is correct but the stance is wrong. Ensure the back leg locks straight at the end of the move and the feet finish hip-width apart. Keep the shoulders square to the front and punch to the centre of the body.

Gyaku Zuki (Reverse Punch)

This is a very powerful punch and one of the more frequently used attacks. Because of its versatility and speed of delivery, it is often used to good effect in freestyle and competition work.

Traditionally, zenkutsu dachi (front stance) is used to teach the technique in the first instance, but gyaku zuki can be used in various other stances. Good hip rotation is essential when executing the punch (Figs 125–129).

Fig 125 Step 1

STEP 1
Assume the left gedan barai position in left zenkutsu dachi.

STEP 2
Without moving the feet or the right fist, move the left open hand up to the right shoulder.

STEP 3
Keeping the feet and right fist where they are, move the left hand to the front and perform a left tate shuto uke (vertical knife hand block) with the hips at hanmi (sideways-on). For training purposes this punch is practised from this starting point.

STEP 4
Keeping the feet where they are, and maintaining a good zenkutsu dachi, punch with the right hand while simultaneously bringing the left hand back to the hip. During the course of the execution of this punch the hips should rotate so that they are square-on to the front on completion.

84

Fig 126 Step 2

Fig 127 Step 3

Fig 128 Step 4 (a)

Fig 129 Step 4 (b)

STEP 5
Return to the left tate shuto uke position and repeat the movement described at Step 3. The punch can then be repeated.

A further method of training for gyaku zuki, once the basics have been mastered, is to punch from a freestyle stance moving into zenkutsu dachi on delivery of the punch. This method is demonstrated in the next sequence of illustrations (Figs 130–132).

STEP 1
Assume a left freestyle stance with the left foot forward and the hands in front of the body to form a guard.

STEP 2
From freestyle stance transfer the weight forward over the front foot, changing into front stance. Perform a right reverse punch while simultaneously bringing the left hand back to the left hip.

STEP 3
Return to the left freestyle stance by transferring the weight back from the front foot. Bring the hands back in front of the body in preparation for repeating the punch.

Common Mistakes
One of the main characteristics of gyaku zuki is the use and rotation of the hips from which

Fig 130 Step 1

Fig 131 Step 2 (a)

Fig 132 Step 2 (b)

Fig 133 Incorrect rotation of hips in which the right hip and shoulder drops

the punch derives its power. With correct technique the whole body is used in the punch, not just the arms and shoulders. Poor or incorrect use of the hips is one of the more common problems associated with this move (Fig 133).

Gyaku zuki is usually executed in zenkutsu dachi. When using zenkutsu dachi the hip rotation will be hindered if the feet are not positioned hip-width apart. A common mistake is for the feet to be in line, which not only creates instability but also restricts the range of hip movement (Fig 134).

The hips and shoulders must also remain level throughout the rotating action and the spine kept upright at all times. Do not lean into the punch.

Tate Zuki (Vertical Punch)

This punch can be performed in the same way as oi zuki (stepping punch) and gyaku zuki (reverse punch). The only difference is

87

Fig 134 Incorrect – rotation of the hip is restricted if the feet are placed in line

Fig 135 Tate zuki

that the punching hand is vertical at the point of impact and has not therefore rotated the full 180 degrees (Fig 135).

Age Zuki (Rising Punch)

Age zuki is similar to choku zuki (straight punch) and oi zuki (stepping punch) except that as the punching hand extends from the hip, it rises in an upward direction. The punch commences in a straight line but starts

to move in an upward direction as the fist starts to rotate. The punch can be very deceptive and often difficult to detect in sufficient time to block effectively.

Ura Zuki (Close Punch)

Ura zuki is a close punch and very powerful in its application. The punching hand only covers a short distance from the hip to the target area but the whole weight of the body can be applied at the moment of impact (Fig 136).

Fig 136 Ura zuki

Fig 137 Step 1

STEP 2
Punch with the right, leading hand, turning the fist 180 degrees while lunging forward. Simultaneously, draw the opposite hand back to the hip. In executing this technique the stance should change from the freestyle stance into zenkutsu dachi (front stance) with the shoulders sideways-on (hanmi). Complete the move by returning to the freestyle stance.

Kizami Zuki (Jabbing Punch)

Kizami zuki is a short, jabbing punch using the leading hand. The punch is generally used as a stunning technique, to set up other counter-attacking moves.

In the example given below, kizami zuki is delivered from a jiyu kumite gamae (freestyle) stance (Figs 137–138).

STEP 1
Assume a right freestyle position with the hands held up in front of the body.

Shuto Uchi (Knife Hand Strike)

Shuto uchi is a strike using the side of the hand. The move is particularly effective when

89

Fig 138 Step 2

aimed at the neck or throat area, although this is not its only application (Fig 139).

Shuto uchi can be performed in two ways. In Version 1, the hand travels in from the outside of the body, in Version 2, the reverse.

Fig 139 Shuto uchi

Version 1 (Figs 140–143)
STEP 1
Assume the yoi (ready) position in heiko dachi (parallel stance) with both hands formed as fists.

STEP 2
Keeping the shoulders square, push the left hand outward in front of the body, straightening the arm while simultaneously raising the right arm up to the side, so that the arm forms a right angle at the elbow. The palm of the hand should be facing outward at this stage.

STEP 3
In a circular movement, start to move the right arm down and across the front of the body while drawing the left hand back towards the hip.

STEP 4
Continue the circular movement with the right arm across the front of the body to complete the strike using the edge of the hand. Draw the left hand back fully to the hip.

The shuto uchi can then be repeated on the opposite side using the left arm to perform the strike. Each arm should then be practised alternately to ensure their equal development.

Version 2 (Figs 144–147)
STEP 1
Again, commence this technique from the yoi position in heiko dachi.

Fig 140 Step 1

Fig 141 Step 2

Fig 142 Step 3

Fig 143 Step 4

Fig 144 Step 1

Fig 145 Step 2

Fig 146 Step 3

Fig 147 Step 4

STEP 2
Keeping the shoulders square, push the left hand outward in front of the body, straightening the arm while simultaneously raising the right hand up to the side of the neck so that the palm of the hand is facing inward. The right hand can be either open or clenched at this point.

STEP 3
In a circular movement, start to move the right hand across the front of the body while drawing the left hand back towards the hip.

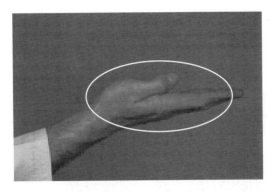

Fig 148 Haito uchi

STEP 4
Continue the circular movement with the right arm across the front of the body to complete the strike using the edge of the hand. Draw the left hand fully to the hip as a fist.

The shuto uchi can then be repeated on the opposite side using the left arm to perform the strike.

Once the hand actions described above have been mastered, the strike can then be practised moving forward and back in the various stances.

Haito Uchi (Ridge Hand Strike)

Haito uchi is a strike using the opposite side of the hand from shuto uchi (knife hand strike). The technique is particularly effective when aimed at the neck or throat area although this is not its only application (Fig 148).

Haito uchi can be performed in two ways. In Version 1, the hand travels in from the outside of the body, in Version 2, the reverse.

Version 1 (Figs 149–152)
STEP 1
Commence from the yoi (ready) position.

STEP 2
Keeping the shoulders square, push the left hand out in front of the body, straightening the left arm. Move the right hand across the body so that the hand is above the left hip with the back of the hand facing upward. The hand can be either open or clenched at this point.

STEP 3
Move the right hand across the body in a circular motion, twisting the hand 180 degrees so that the back of the hand faces downward and strike with the thumb side of the hand. The left arm should simultaneously be brought back to the left hip.

93

Fig 149 Step 1

Fig 150 Step 2

Fig 151 Step 3 (a)

Fig 152 Step 3 (b)

The technique should then be repeated on the opposite side, using the left arm to perform the strike.

Version 2 (Figs 153–155)

STEP 1
Commence from the yoi position. Push the left hand out and bring the right hand back to the hip as a fist.

STEP 2
Move the right hand out from the hip in a small, circular movement to the front. Rotate the hand 180 degrees so that at the end of the move the palm is facing down. At the same time, draw the left hand back to the hip.

Fig 154 Step 2 (a)

Fig 153 Step 1

Fig 155 Step 2 (b)

This method of training should be practised on both sides so that you develop equally effective techniques regardless of the side from which they are delivered (Fig 156). They should also be practised stepping forward and back initially, and as you become more adept, at different angles, the intention being to develop the ability to deliver an attack to any direction.

Fig 156 Striking area of the hand on completion of haito uchi

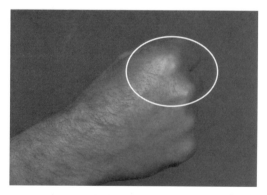

Fig 157 Uraken uchi

Uraken Uchi (Back Fist Strike)

Uraken uchi can be a very fast technique, using the back of the fist to strike the target area. This is an effective technique for striking the temple or side of the head area (Figs 157–160).

STEP 1
Commence from the yoi (ready) position. Move the right hand up to the left shoulder but do not rest on it – this is similar to the

Fig 158 Step 1

start position in gedan barai (downward block). The back of the hand should be positioned so that it is facing outward. The elbow of the right arm should be pointing forward towards the target.

STEP 2
With the right arm pivoting and twisting at the elbow, bring the hand across the front of the body until the arm straightens with the back of the hand facing sideways. Simultaneously, bring the left fist back to the left hip.

Fig 160 Step 2 (b)

The technique should then be repeated on the opposite side using the left arm to perform the strike.

Once this has been achieved, the strike should be practised moving forward and back in the various stances (Fig 161).

Teisho Uchi (Palm Heel Strike)

The weakness in most hand techniques is the wrist, which is prone to buckle on impact if the power is not focused correctly. With

Fig 159 Step 2 (a)

Fig 161 Uraken uchi in zenkutsu dachi

Fig 163 Teisho uchi to the side

teisho uchi this weakness does not apply, making it a particularly useful strike (Fig 162).

Teisho uchi can be applied to either the side or front. It has a variety of applications but is more frequently practised in kiba dachi (horse riding or straddle leg stance) (Fig 163).

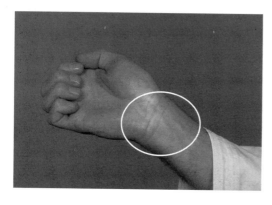

Fig 162 Teisho uchi

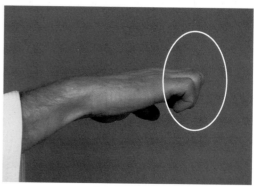

Fig 164 Hiraken uchi

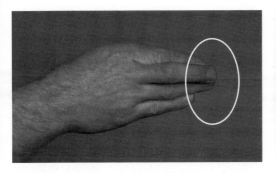

Fig 165 Nukite uchi

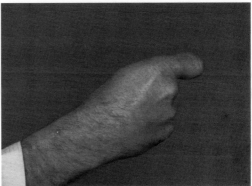

Fig 166 Ippon ken uchi

Hiraken Uchi (Fore Knuckle Strike)

This technique uses the fore knuckles to attack areas such as the throat or bridge of the nose in a straight line. It can be practised in a similar manner to oi zuki (stepping punch) or gyaku zuki (reverse punch) (Fig 164).

Nukite Uchi (Spear Hand Strike)

Nukite uses the tips of the fingers to strike the target area. It is effective when used against soft target areas such as the throat.

As with hiraken uchi (fore knuckle strike), this technique can be practised in a similar manner to oi zuki (stepping punch) or gyaku zuki (reverse punch) (Fig 165).

Ippon Ken Uchi (One Knuckle Strike)

As the name implies, this is a strike using a single knuckle. Conventionally the knuckle used is that of the forefinger (Fig 166).

Nakadaka Ken Uchi (Middle Finger Strike)

Nakadaka ken uchi is similar to ippon ken uchi (one knuckle strike) except that it is the second finger that is used to make the strike. This is the stronger of the two strikes because the knuckle is supported on both sides by the other fingers and can be gripped tight within the fist (Fig 167).

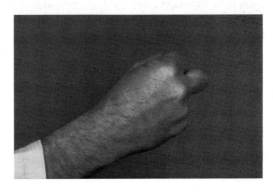

Fig 167 Nakadaka ken uchi

Tetsui Uchi (Bottom Fist Strike)

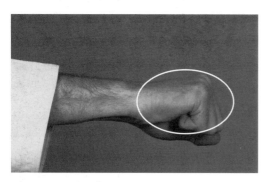

Fig 168 Tetsui uchi

Figs 170–172 Tetsui uchi being used as a strike to the side

Fig 169 Tetsui uchi being used as a downward strike

Fig 171

Fig 172

Tetsui uchi is a strike using the bottom part of the fist and can be used in a number of ways. The most common versions are either as a downward strike or to the side (Figs 168–172).

Nihon Nukite (Two Finger Strike)

Nihon nukite is a strike using two fingers, the index finger and the second finger and can be used to strike the eyes (Fig 173).

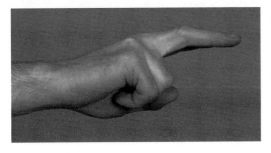

Fig 173 Nihon nukite

Empi Uchi (Elbow Strike)

Fig 174 Age empi uchi (upper elbow strike)

Fig 175 Atoshi empi uchi (downward elbow strike)

Elbow strikes are very effective for close-quarter contact situations. A great deal of speed can be generated over a short distance, making the elbow strike surprisingly powerful and difficult to defend against. There are five types of elbow strikes (Figs 174–178).

Fig 177 Yoko empi uchi (side elbow strike)

Fig 176 Ushiro empi uchi (rear elbow strike)

Fig 178 Mawashi empi uchi (circular elbow strike)

7 Uke (Blocking) Theory and Practice

Blocking is an essential part of any self-defence system. Clearly, if an attack is not effectively stopped or evaded in the first instance, the opportunity to take the initiative and perform the decisive counter-attack may never arise. In general terms, a block entails meeting an attack with sufficient force and in a manner that will deflect or stop it from reaching its target. However, an adept martial artist will also employ other defensive strategies such as evasion, and in extreme cases, pre-emptive attack. There is a saying that 'attack is the best form of defence', and this will always be worthy of consideration. Such a strategy, in many cases, will surprise an opponent and provide a competitive advantage.

Within the karate system there are a number of blocking techniques, each of which have various possible applications. The decision over which block to use will depend upon the individual circumstances of the situation and the amount of time available. Often an instantaneous reaction is required, and choice is a luxury rarely afforded. It is, therefore, necessary to develop the ability to apply a block without thinking, which can only be achieved through regular practice. To this end, the blocks should be practised continuously so that their use becomes second nature.

A block will never realize its full potential if too much reliance is placed on the use of the arms alone. The choice of stance and its correct use are both important factors which, together with good hip movement and focus at the point of impact, will increase the effectiveness of the movement. It is also important to concentrate on maai (correct distancing) and tai sabaki (body movement). Many attacks do not require powerful blocking, which wastes energy, but can be evaded or deflected by simple movement upward, downward or to the sides.

Training in blocking must include practical experience, working with a partner, if satisfactory progress is to be made. Training in this way is the closest most people will get to a real combat situation, and it is important that a high degree of realism enters into this training. The attacks must be strong and on target, yet controlled. The defender must be placed under pressure and made to work, otherwise the training will become meaningless. When training with a partner, however, it is advisable to start off slowly and build up speed as and when ability and confidence allows. Practice at slow speed will assist in training the eye to pick up attacking movements at an early stage.

One final point; it is important not to be misled or blinkered by the term 'block' when using these techniques. All blocks can be used as very effective strikes to vulnerable parts of the body. The angle and direction of strike enables them to reach parts of the body not readily accessible by traditional punches. This concept should be borne in mind at all times.

The blocks taught in the early stages of training involve quite big movements. These blocks have been developed to withstand a strong attack and also serve to develop the body, ensuring the correct muscle action is used. The blocks covered in this chapter are the nine most frequently used which, when mastered, will provide a good defensive repertoire. The blocks covered are:

- Gedan barai (downward block)
- Age uke (upper rising block)
- Uchi ude uke (inside forearm block)
- Soto ude uke (outside forearm block)
- Shuto uke (knife hand block)
- Tate shuto uke (vertical knife hand block)
- Haiwan uke (back arm block)
- Nagashi uke (sweeping block)
- Osae uke (pressing block).

All blocks will be demonstrated from the yoi (ready) position and then move forward in basic stances (Fig 179).

Gedan Barai (Downward Block)

This is normally the first block to be taught. The Japanese word 'barai' translates as parry, which more aptly describes the application, where the attack is parried to one side with the outside of the forearm of the blocking arm. The word 'gedan' means lower level, which again gives an indication to how the technique is to be performed. The blocking arm should travel from the shoulder downward to the lower level of the body (Figs 180–183).

Fig 179 Yoi position

STEP 1

Push out with the left hand and bring the right hand up to the left shoulder, but not resting on it. The back of the hand should be positioned so that it is facing outward; and the elbow of the blocking, right arm, pointing downward.

STEP 2

With the right arm pivoting and twisting at the elbow, move the right hand downward until the arm straightens. Simultaneously, pull the left fist back to the hip rotating the hand so that it ends palm upward.

On completion, the blocking arm should

Fig 181 Step 1 (b)

Fig 180 Step 1 (a)

Fig 182 Step 2 (a)

Fig 183 Step 2 (b)

end up pointing downward, below the hip, so that the back of the hand is facing upward. The timing should be such that the both the blocking and non-blocking arm work together and complete their movement at the same time. The elbow of the non-blocking arm must point backward and not be allowed to stick out to the side (Fig 184).

The block should then be practised on the opposite side using the left hand to perform the block. It is advisable to practise both sides alternately to ensure their equal development.

Having mastered the technique from a static point, the next stage is to perform the

Fig 184 Gedan barai – side view

Fig 185 Step 1 (a)

Fig 186 Step 1 (b)

Fig 187 Step 2

block while stepping forward and back in the various stances. This is demonstrated in the following example using zenkutsu dachi (front stance) (Figs 185–187).

STEP 1

From the yoi (ready) position, step in with the left foot so the feet are together. At the same time, move the left hand up to the right shoulder. Ensure that the elbow is pointing down towards the target, and the left fist is positioned at the shoulder so that the back of the hand is facing outward to the side. Keep the hips square to the front at this stage.

STEP 2

Step out with the left leg into left zenkutsu dachi, ensuring that the feet end up hip-width apart. Simultaneously, block downward with the left hand, pivoting the arm at the elbow, and perform left gedan barai. The blocking hand should end up about 15cm (6in) above the knee, with the right hand withdrawn to the hip. The feet and hands should complete their movement at the same time. On completion of the block the hips should end up sideways-on (hanmi).

In training, all basic blocking, punching and striking techniques usually commence from this left gedan barai position. It is, therefore, worthwhile practising the moves described in Steps 1 and 2 above until the technique can be performed comfortably and with confidence.

Gedan barai is probably the most widely used of the karate blocks and time spent practising will be well rewarded.

The next step is to move forward in zenkutsu dachi, blocking gedan barai with the right hand (Figs 188–192).

STEP 1
Assume the left gedan barai position in zenkutsu dachi.

STEP 2
From this position, step up with the right foot so that both feet are together and the hips are square to the front. Simultaneously, cross the right hand to the left shoulder and push out with the left hand. Keep the back upright and the knees slightly bent throughout this move.

Fig 188 Step 1

Fig 189 Step 2

Fig 190 Step 3

Fig 191 Step 4 (a)

STEP 3

Now step forward with the right foot inscribing an arc so that the feet end up hip-width apart in right zenkutsu dachi. As the foot moves forward, block gedan barai with the right arm so that the hands and feet complete their moves at the same time. As the block is completed the left hip should be pulled back so that the hips finish sideways-on.

STEP 4

This can then be repeated on the opposite side by stepping up and through with the left leg and blocking gedan barai with the left arm.

Common mistakes

The most common mistakes with this block all relate to the hand positioning of the blocking arm both at the start and finish of the technique, and the lack of hip rotation.

At the start of the blocking movement, the hand of the blocking arm should be positioned at the neck so that the back of the hand is facing away to the side. The hand is

Fig 192 Step 4 (b)

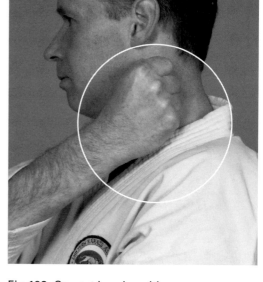

Fig 193 Correct hand position

often incorrectly positioned with the back pointing upward. Do not rest the hand on the shoulder (Figs 193–194).

At the completion of the move, the blocking hand should end up approximately 15cm (6in) above the knee. The tendency at this point is to block too high and too wide. The hips must rotate from square-on at the commencement of the move, to sideways-on at its conclusion.

A further point to bear in mind is the position of the elbow at the start of the block, which should point down in the direction the hand is going to travel. This will ensure that the block takes the shortest and fastest route to the target, avoiding any unnecessary circular movements.

Age Uke (Upper Rising Block)

Age uke is traditionally used to defend against an attack that is being directed towards the head or upper body (jodan).

110

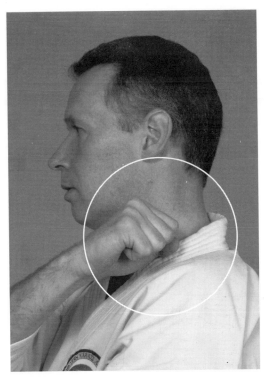

Fig 194 Incorrect hand position

The part of the arm used in the block is the outer part of the forearm.

Age uke is also an effective striking technique that can be targeted at the face, chin or neck area of an attacker (Figs 195–199).

STEP 1

From the yoi (ready) position, draw the right hand to the hip. At the same time, pull the left hand back to the stomach and then push it forward in an upward direction, level with the head.

STEP 2

Start moving the blocking, right hand across the front of the body, simultaneously pulling the left hand back so they cross at the chest with the blocking arm in front.

STEP 3

Continue in an upward direction with the blocking arm, at the same time twisting the forearm so it finishes above the head with the back of the hand facing to the rear. The outside edge of the forearm should now be in place and used as the blocking or striking point on the arm. The non-blocking

Fig 195 Step 1 (a)

Fig 196 Step 1 (b)

Fig 197 Step 1 (c)

Fig 198 Step 2

Fig 199 Step 3

hand should be withdrawn to the hip, palm upward.

The block can then be practised using the opposite arm, progressing to alternately moving from one side to the next.

At the conclusion of this technique, the blocking arm must be far enough above the forehead to effectively defend against a punch to the face (Fig 200). The angle of the blocking arm at the elbow must be greater than 90 degrees. Anything less will weaken the technique.

The next stage is to practise the block while moving forward and back in different stances. Traditionally, age uke is used from zenkutsu dachi (front stance), which is how it is demonstrated in the example below (Figs 201–205).

STEP 1
Commence by stepping into a left gedan barai (downward block) in zenkutsu dachi.

STEP 2
From left gedan barai, step forward with the right foot to meet the left foot in the centre.

Fig 200

Fig 201 Step 1

Fig 202 Step 2

Fig 203 Step 3

Fig 204 Step 4

Fig 205 Step 4 – side view

At the same time, draw the left hand back to the stomach and then push it out and away. The hips should be square-on to the front.

STEP 3
Step half a pace forward with the right foot, ready to complete right zenkutsu dachi. As the foot slides forward, cross the forearms at chest height with the blocking arm in front. Keep the hips square-on at this stage.

STEP 4
Continue forward with the right foot completing a full zenkutsu dachi, ensuring that the feet are hip-width apart, the back leg locked straight, and the front knee bent. Simultaneously, complete a right age uke and draw the left hand back to the hip. As the blocking action is completed, the hips must rotate to hanmi (sideways-on).

Common mistakes
Again, poor stances and failure to use the hips are problems encountered with age uke. Additionally, the position of the blocking arm during and at the end of the movement is often incorrect.

The majority of karate techniques are designed to take the shortest and quickest route to the target area. With age uke, the blocking hand needs to be driven upward, straight from the hip, in front of the chest, to its final position above the head. One of the most frequent mistakes is to add an additional, unnecessary move: this is where the hand of the blocking arm, instead of starting on its upward journey from the hip, is incorrectly drawn across the front of the stomach. If this happens, the blocking hand then needs

Fig 206 Incorrect hand position

to roll up in front of the chest to its final position, which makes the whole move much slower (Fig 206).

Two further mistakes relate to the position of the blocking arm at the end of the move. First, if the blocking arm is too bent, it weakens the technique and can also obscure vision. Second, if the blocking arm finishes too far from the head, it again weakens the technique (Figs 207–208).

115

Fig 207 Incorrect – arm is too bent

Fig 208 Incorrect – arm is too far from the head

Uchi Ude Uke (Inside Forearm Block)

Uchi ude uke can be used to defend against an attack being delivered to either the head, chest or stomach areas. When performed correctly it is very powerful and often used against kicking techniques.

The blocking surface is normally taught as the edge of the forearm (thumb side) and this is how it should be practised under normal circumstances. This will be effective as a defence against arm attacks, but not advisable for blocking kicks. The bone on the thumb side of the forearm (the radius) is small and weak in comparison with the bones of the leg, and strong contact could result in injury. When blocking kicking techniques, the whole of the back of the forearm (haiwan) should be used.

As a striking technique, uchi uke can be effective when targeted towards the body, neck and face using either the forearm or hand as the point of contact.

In the example below, right uchi uke is demonstrated starting from the yoi (ready) position. The block is broken down into three stages (Figs 209–212).

STEP 1

Keeping the shoulders square, push the left hand outward in front of the body, straightening the arm. The hand should open and face palm downward. At the same time, draw the right hand across the body to the left hip with the back of the hand facing upward.

STEP 2

In a circular movement, start to bring the right hand across the body, pivoting at the elbow, while pulling the left, non-blocking arm back towards the hip.

STEP 3

Continuing in a circular movement, bring the right hand across the body, twisting the hand 180 degrees so that the back of the hand faces away, blocking with the outer edge of the forearm. The left hand should now be fully withdrawn to the hip.

On completion of this block, the fist of the

Fig 209 Yoi position

Fig 210 Step 1

117

Fig 211 Step 2

Fig 212 Step 3

blocking arm should be level with the shoulder and a right angle formed at the elbow (Fig 213).

The block should then be repeated on the opposite side, using the left hand to perform the block.

The next stage is to practise the block moving forward and back in the various stances. In the example below zenkutsu dachi (front stance) will again be used (Figs 214–218).

STEP 1
Commence by stepping forward into left gedan barai in zenkutsu dachi.

Fig 213 Correct hand placement – side view

Fig 214 Step 1

Fig 215 Step 2

STEP 2

From the zenkutsu dachi position, step forward with the right foot to meet the left foot in the centre. At the same time, push out with the left hand so that the palm is facing downward and move the right forearm across to the left hip. The back of this fist should be facing upward. At this point, ensure that the hips remain square to the front.

STEP 3

Stepping forward half a pace with the right foot, cross the arms in front of the chest with the blocking arm in front. Again, at this point, the hips should remain square to the front.

STEP 4

Move the right foot forward into a full zenkutsu dachi, ensuring the feet end up hip-width apart, while simultaneously twisting the right forearm to perform the uchi uke (inside forearm block). The non-blocking hand at this point must be pulled back to the hip. As the block is completed, the hips must

Fig 216 Step 3

Fig 217 Step 4

rotate sideways so that the left hip is pulled backward.

After completing the block with right arm, step forward again and practise the opposite side. The block can also be performed on the retreat by stepping backward with the front foot and reversing the moves described above.

Common Mistakes
The most common mistake with uchi uke is the hand placement at the halfway stage.

Instead of the hand facing palm downward, the tendency is to hug the body, with the back of the hand facing outward (Fig 219).

A further point to watch is the scope of the block. Do not block too wide or high as this creates too big a movement and will waste energy. The body must be kept under control at all times (Fig 220).

120

Fig 218 Step 4 – side view

Fig 219 Incorrect hand placement

Soto Ude Uke (Outside Forearm Block)

Soto ude uke can be used to defend against an attack to the head or mid-section of the body. It is a powerful block and can also be effective in striking applications, for instance when striking against the elbow during a breaking technique. Because of the angle and direction of strike, the effective target areas are the neck and face, particularly the sides.

The block, as the name implies, moves from the outside of the body in towards the centre. Concentration should be on correct hand positioning at the start and finish of the

Fig 220 Incorrect – hand too high and wide

Fig 221 Yoi position

Fig 222 Step 1

Fig 223 Step 2

Fig 224 Step 3

movement. The blocking surface is tradition-ally taught as the outside (small finger side) of the forearm, which is how it should be practised (Figs 221–224).

STEP 1

From the yoi (ready) position and keeping the shoulders square, push the left, open hand out to the front, straightening the arm so it ends up palm downward. At the same time, move the right arm, keeping it as a fist, up to the side so that the upper arm is parallel to the ground and a right angle forms at the elbow. The palm of the hand should be facing out to the side.

STEP 2

In a circular movement, start to bring the right hand down across the front of the body. The left hand should commence its journey back to the hip.

STEP 3

Continuing the circular movement, bring the blocking arm across the front of the body, pivoting at the elbow, so that the blocking arm ends with the back of the arm facing away.

On completion of this technique, the fist of the blocking arm should be at shoulder height, level with the opposite shoulder. The elbow should form a right angle. If the little finger is tensed at the end of the technique, it will aid the tensing of the muscles in the forearm on impact (Fig 225).

As with the other blocks, soto ude uke should be practised on both the right and left side to ensure equal development of the technique.

Fig 225 Correct hand position

Once this block can be performed with both the right and left arms from the static position, progression should be to blocking while stepping forward and back in the various stances. Again, soto ude uke is traditionally practised in zenkutsu dachi (front stance), which is how it is demonstrated in the example below (Figs 226–230).

STEP 1

Commence from gedan barai (downward block) in zenkutsu dachi. The hips should be sideways-on, facing at an angle of 45 degrees.

Fig 226 Step 1

Fig 227 Step 2

Fig 228 Step 3

Fig 229 Step 4

STEP 2

Step forward with the rear (right) foot until the feet are positioned together. At the same time, push the left hand forward and bring the right fisted-hand out to the side so that the palm of the hand is facing outward and a right angle is formed at the elbow.

STEP 3

Step forward half a pace with the right foot, and commence rotating the blocking arm across the front of the body, drawing the non-blocking arm back towards the hip. The hips should still be facing forward, square-on, at this point.

STEP 4

Slide forward with the right foot into a full zenkutsu dachi and simultaneously perform a right outside forearm block. As the block is executed, the hips should rotate so that they end up facing sideways-on.

This method of training should be practised on alternate sides to ensure their equal development. It should also be practised stepping back, reversing the steps described above.

Common Mistakes
Excluding bad stances and lack of hip movement, the most common mistakes in performing soto ude uke relate to hand and

Fig 230 Step 4 – side view

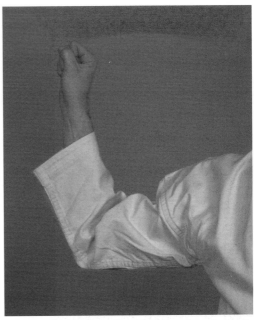

Fig 231 Correct – wrist straight

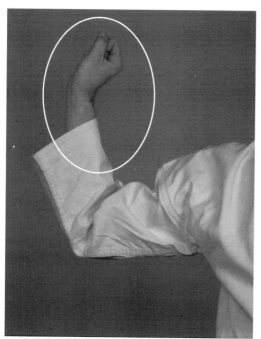

Fig 233 Incorrect – arm is positioned too low

Fig 232 Incorrect – wrist bent

arm positioning at the start and finish of the block.

It is important to ensure that the wrist is kept straight throughout the blocking technique. A common mistake is for it to bend in or out when the hand is moved up to the side at the start of the block (Figs 231–232).

When the hand is at the side, the upper arm must be parallel to the ground and a right angle formed at the elbow. A common mistake at this point is to allow the blocking arm to drop at the shoulder and bend too far at the elbow (Fig 233).

At the completion of block, ensure that the

Fig 234 Incorrect – arm has not cleared chest area

126

arm has moved far enough across the body to clear the chest area. A common mistake is to leave the arm short so that the chest is still exposed. Quite obviously this would be ineffective as a blocking technique. Be careful when checking this – it is possible that the problem actually lies with the hips, which have not rotated sufficiently to allow the arm to cross the chest (Fig 234).

Shuto Uke (Knife Hand Block)

Shuto uke can be used to defend against attacks being directed at either the head, chest or stomach areas. It can also be used as an effective strike to vital points on the attacker's arm or neck. The part of the hand used in the block is the outer edge, just above the wrist.

When performing the block, it is important to avoid opening the fingers, and the thumb of the blocking hand should be tucked in to avoid injury.

Shuto uke is an awkward block to perform at first, with quite a lot to think about. The block is traditionally practised moving in kokutsu dachi (back stance), which adds to the difficulty factor, as this is also awkward and unnatural in the early stages of training. It is important not to rush this block but take time to concentrate on the more intricate parts. It will require a lot of practice before the block becomes comfortable and can be used with confidence.

It is not easy to perform shuto uke from a static position. For this reason, the block is demonstrated stepping forward into kokutsu dachi (Figs 235–240).

Fig 235 Step 1

STEP 1
The block should commence from the yoi (ready) position in heiko dachi (parallel stance), with both hands formed as fists.

STEP 2
Keeping the shoulders square, bring the feet together by moving the left foot in to join the right. Push the right hand outward in front of the body, straightening the right arm. Simultaneously, bring the left hand up to the right shoulder.

127

Fig 236 Step 2

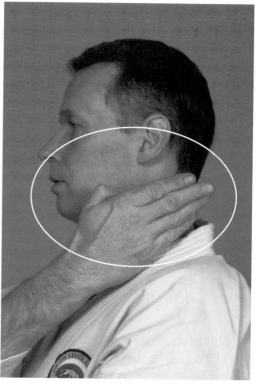

Fig 237 Step 2 – correct hand position

The left hand at the shoulder should be open handed, and the palm facing inward. The left elbow should be pointing in the direction of travel, and the hips square.

STEP 3
With the left leg, step forward half a pace in a straight line. Start to bring the left hand down across the chest while withdrawing the right hand.

STEP 4
Step forward with the left leg, completing kokutsu dachi. At the same time, in a circular movement, bring the left hand across the front of the body, blocking with the outer edge of the hand. Simultaneously, move the right hand back to the stomach with the palm facing upward so it is positioned just above the belt.

128

Fig 238 Step 3

Fig 239 Step 4

At the conclusion of this block, the hips must be sideways-on and the blocking arm bent at the elbow to form a right angle. It is important that the non-blocking hand stays open and does not return to the hip, but finishes at the centre of the stomach, above the belt.

Generally, all basic combinations that include shuto uke start from this left shuto uke position in kokutsu dachi. Therefore, it is advisable to practise the single technique described above until it can be performed with confidence.

Having developed the ability to perform shuto uke as a single move, the block should then be repeated using the opposite hand while stepping forward in kokutsu dachi (Figs 241–244).

129

Fig 240 Step 4 – side view

Fig 241 Step 1

STEP 1

Commence this sequence of moves from a left shuto uke position in kokutsu dachi.

STEP 2

Step up with the rear leg so that the feet are together. At the same time, straighten the left arm, keeping the hand open with the palm facing downward, and move the right hand up to the left shoulder with the hand open and positioned so that the palm is facing inward.

STEP 3

With the right leg, step forward half a pace in a straight line. Start to bring the right hand down across the chest and withdraw the left hand.

STEP 4

Step forward with the right leg to complete kokutsu dachi. At the same time, in a circular movement, bring the right hand across the front of the body and block with the outer

130

Fig 243 Step 3

Fig 242 Step 2

edge of the hand. Simultaneously, bring the left hand back to the stomach with the palm facing upward.

Common Mistakes
Although shuto uke is quite a difficult block to get to grips with, there are a number of frequent mistakes that can be corrected fairly

easily, resulting in a much better blocking or striking action.

When positioning the blocking hand at the neck, check that the hand is sideways-on, with the palm facing the neck. A common mistake is to have the palm facing down towards the shoulder (Fig 245).

At the conclusion of the block, the non-blocking hand should be positioned at the

131

Fig 244 Step 4

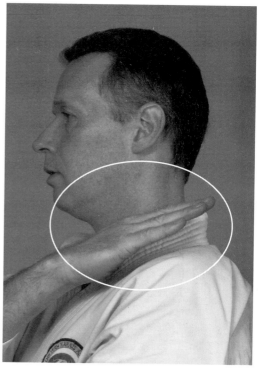

Fig 245 Incorrect hand placement

stomach with the palm facing up: a frequent mistake is to have the hand hugging the stomach, with the palm facing inward (Fig 246).

The blocking arm at the end of the technique must be bent and the top of the hand level with the shoulder. Often this is performed with the blocking arm too straight (Fig 247).

Keep the back upright throughout the blocking action and avoid the temptation to lean back into the technique (Fig 248).

General Considerations

The blocks covered so far are the five most frequently used blocks in traditional karate styles. These are taught from a very early stage, and remain part of the training regime regardless of grade. They also feature widely in pre-determined kumite (sparring) exercises such as gohon and kihon ippon kumite (five and one attack sparring); and in basic, intermediate and advanced kata. The importance of practising the blocks and concentrating on the finer details is, therefore, self-evident.

Fig 246 Incorrect hand position at the waist

Fig 247 Incorrect – blocking arm is too straight

Fig 248 Incorrect – leaning back too far

One or more of the following factors will determine the type of block and approach adopted:

- How much thinking time is available?
- What direction is the attack coming from?
- How much force is needed to defend?
- Can the attack be deflected or must it be met full on?
- Can the attack be evaded without the need to block at all?
- Is the best approach to step into the attack, closing the attacker down, or is it more practical to move away while blocking?
- What counter-attack will be used?

Specific aspects and common mistakes were covered in some detail with the individual blocking techniques. There are, however, a number of facets that are general to all five blocks. Some have been mentioned previously and are revisited here; others will be dealt with for the first time.

133

It is these issues that will determine which block is to be used, and how much power is to be applied in defence. Clearly, there is plenty to think about and possibly with only a split second of time available. So how is this possible? The response has to be automatic, and this ability to react almost without thinking can only be achieved if the blocking techniques are practised repetitively and laboriously on both sides of the body. This can never be overstated.

Whichever block or counter-attack is used, it is important that it is delivered from a strong base with good balance and stability. Stance selection and application is an integral part of the blocking technique. It is this aspect that is often overlooked or ignored. Good blocks must be accompanied by good stances.

When moving in the various stances, the hips must be kept level throughout the move, and the back maintained in an upright position. In order to move quickly, the body has to remain relaxed throughout the

Fig 249 Step 1

Fig 250 Step 2

134

blocking action, only tensing for a split second at the point of contact.

All the five blocks discussed so far involve the use of the hips during the movement. At no time do the blocks rely on the use of the arms alone. Through correct application of the hips, legs, back, and stomach muscles, the whole body is used and comes together as one at the end of the move.

Remember – blocking techniques can also be used to strike vital or vulnerable parts of the body, they must never be considered purely as blocks.

The five blocks considered above should initially be practised from a static position, concentrating on the arm movements alone. Progress can then be made to performing the blocks while moving forward and back in the various stances.

Tate Shuto Uke (Vertical Knife Hand Block)

Tate shuto uke is similar to the previous shuto uke block, using the same part of

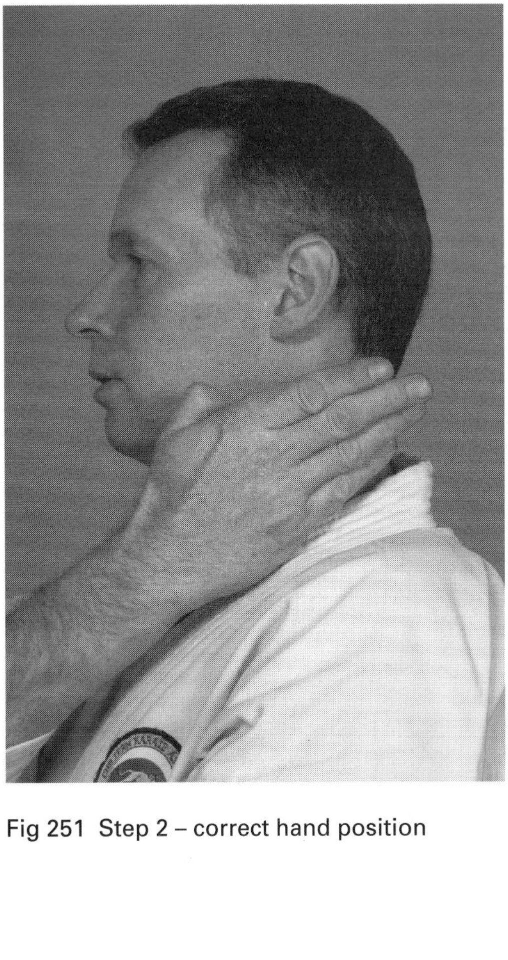

Fig 251 Step 2 – correct hand position

Fig 252 Step 3

135

Fig 254 Haiwan uke chudan

Fig 253 Haiwan uke jodan

the hand, the outer edge. It can be used to block against an attack towards the head, chest or stomach, and can also be a good striking technique, attacking the arms and neck area.

When performing this block, the arm of the blocking hand must be straight, and the hand bent at the wrist so that it forms as near to a right angle as possible (Figs 249–252).

STEP 1
Commence in a left gedan barai (downward block) position in zenkutsu dachi (front stance).

STEP 2
Move the left hand up to the right shoulder. The hand should be open with the palm facing inward, and the elbow pointing in the direction of travel.

STEP 3
In a circular movement, bring the left hand across the front of the body so that the arm straightens, blocking with the outer edge of the hand.

Fig 255 Nagashi uke

Fig 256 Osae uke

Haiwan Uke (Back Arm Block)

Haiwan uke is a relatively strong block using the back of the arm. It can be used either to block an attack to the upper body (jodan) or lower body (gedan) (Figs 253–254).

Nagashi Uke (Sweeping Block)

Nagashi uke is one of a number of blocks that uses the palm of the hand. It can be an effec- tive block across the front of the body from either side and is generally used against an attack to the upper body (Fig 255).

Osae Uke (Pressing Block)

Like nagashi uke (sweeping block), this block uses the palm of the hand. 'Osae' means pressing and this block is used to push down- ward, in defence (Fig 256).

8 Geri (Kicking) Theory and Practice

Geri (kicking) techniques form an important and fundamental part of the karate system and, when executed correctly, can have a devastating and decisive effect. However, the kicks must be used wisely and never practised to the neglect of the other weapons in the armoury. A well-structured karate syllabus will take this into account and cover all aspects of training, providing a complete system in which all the elements come together as one.

This 'complete system' is an important concept because kicks, although powerful, will never be as fast as the hands, and are restricted to application from a distance. Once the confrontation becomes 'close quarter', the ability to use kicks is severely reduced and, in most cases, the hands, arms and other parts of the body must take over.

To maximize the effectiveness of the kicking action, the whole body must be used, bringing into play the muscles in both the kicking and supporting legs, and also the buttocks, hips, stomach and back. The muscles must act in harmony, which requires flexibility and fluidity of movement. This, in turn, will aid the delivery of the kicks, which can only be performed while balancing on one leg with much reduced stability. Maai (correct distancing), kime (focus) and zanshin (awareness) are also important for effective kicks, without which the techniques would fail to realize their full potential.

When practising the various kicks, it should be taken into account that the power applied will be influenced by the distance the foot travels, and the speed generated through the move. The further the foot can travel, the greater the opportunity to build up speed and power. The distance covered by a kick can be increased by correct placement of the knee at the intermediate stage, which is an area covered in some detail in the next few pages.

The kicking action employed in the majority of kicks is quite complex and will sometimes require unnatural body movement. Difficulties in kicking techniques frequently arise from incorrect body action and not from lack of flexibility, which is often thought to be the case. For example, in kekomi (side thrust kick), the range of the kick will be shortened if the supporting foot does not turn correctly (180 degrees) during the kick. Additionally, failure to achieve the correct rotation of the supporting foot will place stress on the hip joint, leading to injury.

If a joint is forced to move beyond its natural range with any degree of speed, the result can be catastrophic. This point is highlighted in the hope that it will encourage emphasis to be placed on achieving correct body movement, thereby reducing the risk of injury while increasing the power and effectiveness of the kick. It is advisable to practise each kick slowly at first, allowing the body to become accustomed to the required range of movement. Concentration should be on the quality of technique rather than speed and power, which can be gradually increased without risk of injury once the kick can be performed comfortably.

One method of training is to practise the kicks while wearing ankle weights. This must be done slowly: the slower the movement, the greater the benefit will be. This is not a new training concept – the karate students in Okinawa 150 years ago would practise their kicks while wearing ishi-geta (metal and stone shoes).

In the following pages, a lot of emphasis will be placed on the supporting, non-kicking leg. During the early stages of training, the role of this leg is often overlooked or neglected. However, it is just as important, if not more so, than the kicking leg. Failure to grasp the correct movement will result in poor kicks and could cause injury. Please bear this in mind at all times.

The kicks covered in this chapter are:

- Mae geri (front kick)
- Yoko geri keage (side snap kick)
- Yoko geri kekomi (side thrust kick)
- Mawashi geri (roundhouse kick)
- Ushiro geri (back kick)

- Mikazuki geri (crescent kick)
- Gyaku mawashi geri (inside roundhouse kick)
- Ushiro mawashi geri (reverse roundhouse kick)
- Kakato geri (axe kick)
- Ashi barai (sweeping kick)
- Fumikomi (stamping kick)
- Hiza geri (knee kick).

The theory covered in respect of these kicks will be based on traditional karate applications that differ somewhat from the sport karate approach. Remember that height is not important, the majority of kicks can be delivered with optimum power at hip level.

Try not to lose heart when practising the techniques: the kicks will only be mastered with devotion of time, effort and patience.

Mae Geri (Front Kick)

Mae geri is normally the first kick to be taught because it is probably the easiest to learn and the most natural. Once perfected, the kick can be delivered with extreme speed and devastating power, making it one of the most effective self-defence techniques.

The kick comes in two forms: mae geri keage (snap kick), which is how it is usually taught, and mae geri kekomi (thrust kick). The thrust kick is the stronger of the two, in which the full power of the hips is used.

Mae Geri from a Static Position

It is advisable to commence practising mae geri from heiko dachi (parallel stance). Concentrate on correct leg positioning and movement (Figs 257–262).

Fig 257 Heiko dachi – front view

Fig 258 Heiko dachi – side view

STEP 1

From the start position in heiko dachi, bring the right knee up in front of the body while ensuring that the foot of the kicking leg remains parallel to the ground with the toes pulled back. The supporting leg should remain slightly bent at the knee to aid stability and balance. At this point, the foot of the supporting leg can either remain pointing forward or turn out 45 degrees to the side for greater stability, but should remain firmly in contact with the floor.

STEP 2

Extend the kicking leg so that it straightens at the knee in a direct line with the centre of the body, keeping the back upright at all times. Pull the toes back so that the ball of the foot becomes the striking surface.

Fig 259 Step 1

Fig 260 Step 2

Fig 261 Step 3

STEP 3
Return the kicking leg to the position described at Step 1 above.

STEP 4
Having completed the kick, return the foot of the kicking leg to the ground in heiko dachi.

The kick should then be practised on the opposite side following Steps 1 to 4 above, using the left leg as the kicking leg.

Stepping Forward
Having grasped the essentials from a static position, mae geri can then be practised from zenkutsu dachi (front stance), stepping forward after each kick.

Commence by assuming a zenkutsu dachi

Fig 262 Step 4

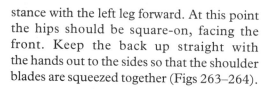

Fig 263 Zenkutsu dachi

Fig 264 Zenkutsu dachi – side view

stance with the left leg forward. At this point the hips should be square-on, facing the front. Keep the back up straight with the hands out to the sides so that the shoulder blades are squeezed together (Figs 263–264).

STEP 1

From the start position in zenkutsu dachi, bring the right knee up in front of the body. At the same time, ensure that the foot of the kicking leg remains parallel to the ground with the toes pulled back.

STEP 2

Extend the kicking leg so that it straightens at the knee in a direct line with the centre of the body, keeping the back upright.

STEP 3

Return the kicking leg to the position described at Step 1 above.

STEP 4

Having completed the kick, step forward with the kicking leg into zenkutsu dachi, ensuring that the foot lands so that the feet are hip-width apart in the stance.

Fig 265 Step 1

Fig 266 Step 2

Fig 267 Step 3

Fig 268 Step 4

The kick should then be practised on the opposite side following Steps 1 to 4 above, using the left leg as the kicking leg.

When performing this kick it is very important to keep the supporting leg slightly bent to aid balance and stability, and to keep the back as upright as possible. The kicking action must be developed so that it becomes a fast, snapping kick using the ball of the foot.

Mae Geri Kekomi (Thrust Kick)

The training method for mae geri kekomi is the same as the snap kick version except that the power of the hips comes into play. As the kicking leg extends, the hips should thrust forward, locking the leg on impact with the target. The hips must be kept square-on to the front throughout this kick (Fig 269).

Common Mistakes

On the face of it, the mae geri kick looks straightforward and fairly easy to perform. This, however, is not always the case and a number of finer points are often missed or neglected.

When the knee of the kicking leg is lifted off the ground towards the chest, a common mistake is for the toes to be pointing downward as opposed to the correct position, which is parallel to the ground (Fig 270).

Fig 270 Incorrect – toes should not point downward

Fig 269 Mae geri kekomi

The kicking position of the foot also causes problems with some people. Remember it is the ball of the foot that should make contact with the target, not the toes. Also, take care not to kick with the toes pointing upward at the point of impact; the ball of the foot must penetrate into the target in a straight line.

When performing the snapping version of this kick, it is important to keep the back as upright as possible. It is a common mistake to lean either backward or forward. This is not conducive to good stability and will restrict the application and power of the kick. Similarly, when the kicking leg is extended, the back must remain straight, avoiding the tendency to lean back (Figs 271–273).

A further common mistake is for the foot of the supporting leg to be raised as the kicking leg extends. This will affect balance, stability and ultimately the power of the kick. The risk of this occurring increases with the height of the kick, as over-stretching causes the foot to rise (Fig 274).

Fig 271 Incorrect – leaning backward

Fig 272 Incorrect – leaning forward

Fig 273 Incorrect kicking position

Fig 274 Incorrect – foot should remain on the ground

In advanced applications of mae geri, the striking point of the foot can be changed to include the toes, instep or heel of the foot as circumstances dictate.

Yoko Geri Keage (Side Snap Kick)

Yoko geri keage is a side kick which, like mae geri keage, must be developed so that it can be executed quickly in a snapping action. This particular kick will need a great deal of practice before it will become effective.

Yoko Geri Keage from a Static Position

Initially, it is advisable to practise the kick from heiko dachi (parallel stance), concentrating on correct leg positioning and movement (Figs 275–278).

STEP 1

From the start position in heiko dachi, turn the head to the left and raise the left knee up

146

Fig 276 Step 1

Fig 275 Heiko dachi

to the side so that the knee is pointing towards the intended target. Keep the supporting leg slightly bent at the knee to aid stability and balance. Ensure that the foot of the supporting leg remains fully in contact with the floor at all times throughout this kick.

STEP 2
Pivoting at the knee, snap the kicking foot out and in an upward direction, using the instep as the striking point of the foot.

STEP 3
Quickly return the kicking foot to the side and resume the position described at Step 1, then return the foot to the ground in heiko dachi.

Steps 1 to 3 above should then be repeated using the opposite leg.

147

Fig 277 Step 2

Fig 279 Step 1

Stepping to the Side
Once the kick can be performed with confidence, it can then be practised moving forward and back in kiba dachi (horse riding or straddle leg stance) and the other karate stances (Figs 279–284).

Fig 278 Step 3

Fig 280 Step 2

Fig 281 Step 3

STEP 1

Assume a kiba dachi stance facing the left. Keep the back upright and pull the arms back so that the shoulder blades are squeezed together.

STEP 2

Keeping the hands where they are and the back upright, step over the left foot with the right.

STEP 3

Raise the left knee up to the side so that the knee is pointing towards the intended target. Keep the supporting leg slightly bent at the knee to aid stability and balance.

STEP 4

Pivoting at the knee, snap the kicking foot out in an upward direction using the instep as the striking point of the foot.

149

Fig 282 Step 4

Fig 283 Step 5 (a)

STEP 5
Quickly return the kicking foot to the side and resume the position described at Step 3, then return the foot to the ground in kiba dachi.

Steps 1 to 5 above can also be practised in the opposite direction, kicking with the right leg.

Common Mistakes
Yoko geri keage is a very awkward kick to perform, which can cause problems resulting in a weak kick. It will require a lot of practice and perseverance.

The most common mistake concerns the position of the foot at the point of impact. Often the toes and foot of the kicking leg end up pointing upward, making it impossible to make contact with the side and/or instep of the foot (Fig 285).

Other mistakes include not snapping the kick and leaving the foot in place too long. Also, the failure to return the kicking foot to the side before stepping back down into kiba dachi reduces the ability to perform multiple kicks with the same leg.

Fig 284 Step 5 (b)

Fig 285 Incorrect kicking position with toe pointing up

Yoko Geri Kekomi (Side Thrust Kick)

Yoko geri kekomi is a side thrust kick which, when performed correctly, is probably the most powerful of all the karate kicks. It is, however, one of the hardest kicks to learn and usually the one that causes most difficulty.

At first, it is advisable to practise the kick slowly and with care, as an incorrect kicking action can place a lot of stress on the hip joint. Pay particular attention to the action of the supporting leg which is equally, if not more important than that of the kicking leg (Fig 286).

Yoko Geri Kekomi from a Static Position

As with the side snap kick, commence by practising from heiko dachi (parallel stance), concentrating on correct leg movement (Figs 287–290). Once this has been achieved,

151

Fig 286 Yoko geri kekomi

Fig 287 Step 1

progress can be made towards performing the kick from kiba dachi (horse riding or straddle leg stance) and zenkutsu dachi (front stance).

STEP 1

From the start position in heiko dachi, raise the left knee up so that the knee is pointing towards the front. At this point, bend the knee so that the heel of the kicking foot is tucked in and level with the inside of the supporting leg. Keep the supporting leg slightly bent at the knee to aid stability and balance. Ensure that the foot of the supporting leg remains fully in contact with the floor at all times throughout the kick.

STEP 2

Start to move the kicking foot out to the side, ensuring the heel of the kicking foot moves in a straight line towards the intended target. At this point the supporting foot must start to pivot in the opposite direction. This will open the hip up and allow the kicking leg to extend more freely.

STEP 3

Continue extending the kicking leg until it locks out straight at the side. At the completion of the kick, the foot of the supporting

Fig 288 Step 2

Fig 289 Step 3

leg must have pivoted a full 90 degrees from its start position, so that it ends up pointing in the opposite direction to the kicking leg. The striking surface of the foot is the outside edge of the heel. This ensures that the bones of the kicking leg are straight on impact.

When practicing yoko geri kekomi in training, it is beneficial to hold the kick in the final 'locked' position for a split second. This will help ensure that the kick thrusts out rather than becoming a snapping action.

STEP 4
Quickly return the kicking foot to the side, resume the initial start position, and then return the foot to the ground in heiko dachi.

Fig 290 Step 4

Steps 1 to 3 above should then be repeated using the opposite leg.

Stepping to the Side
Once the kick can be performed with confidence from a static position it can be practised moving forward and back in kiba dachi and the other karate stances (Figs 291–296).

STEP 1
Assume a kiba dachi stance facing the left. Keep the back upright and pull the arms back so that the shoulder blades are squeezed together.

STEP 2
Keeping the hands where they are and the back upright, step over with the right foot.

Fig 291 Step 1

Fig 292 Step 2

Fig 293 Step 3

Fig 294 Step 4

STEP 3

Raise the left knee up so that the knee is pointing towards the front. Remember to keep the foot of the supporting leg fully in contact with the floor throughout the kick, and keep looking towards the target.

STEP 4

Start to move the kicking foot out to the side, ensuring the heel of the kicking foot moves in a straight line towards the intended target. At the same time, start to pivot the supporting foot.

STEP 5

Complete the kick by extending the kicking leg until it locks out straight at the side, ensuring the foot of the supporting leg has pivoted the full 90 degrees from its start position.

STEP 6

Return the kicking foot to the side and resume the initial start position. Return the foot to the ground in kiba dachi.

Fig 295 Step 5

Fig 296 Step 6

Common Mistakes

Generally, yoko geri kekomi is introduced at a very early stage in training, and often causes a number of problems if the correct kicking action is not understood. It must always be remembered that this is probably the hardest karate kick to master, requiring unnatural body movement.

When the kick is first taught, the action of the supporting leg is just as important, if not more so, than the actual kicking leg. As described above, the supporting foot must pivot so that it is pointing away from the target at completion of the kick, releasing pressure on the hip joint and enabling the kicking leg to extend out to the side. Failure to perfect this action could result in injury to the hip joint if the kick is performed incorrectly and at speed: this is, perhaps, the most common mistake. Therefore, it is advisable to concentrate on perfecting this aspect of the kick slowly at first, as it is all a matter of timing.

The photograph (Fig 297) shows the intermediate position with the supporting foot starting to pivot as the kicking leg is moving out to the side.

The next photograph (Fig 298) shows the

Fig 297 Kekami – intermediate position

Fig 298 Supporting foot facing the opposite direction to the kick on completion

position at the completion of the kicking action, with the supporting foot pointing in the opposite direction to the kick.

When performing this kick, keep the supporting leg slightly bent to aid balance and stability. The back should be as upright as possible at all times, resisting the temptation to lean back, away from the direction of the kick.

At the halfway stage, the heel of the kicking leg needs to be in line with the inside of the supporting leg. This helps to ensure that when the leg is extended in the kick, the heel of the foot travels in a straight line, taking the fastest route to the target (Fig 299).

Another mistake when performing kekomi is the failure to extend the kicking leg fully. The tendency is to snap the foot back instead of locking the leg out on completion of the kick. If necessary, practise the kick aimed at knee level rather than being too ambitious at first. This will help develop correct kicking action: the height can be increased over time.

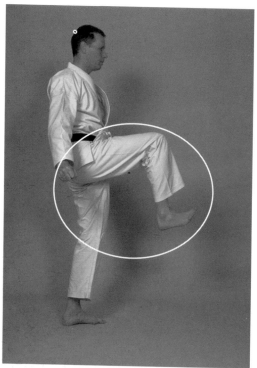

Fig 299 Incorrect – heel not in line with supporting leg

Mawashi Geri (Roundhouse Kick)

Mawashi geri uses the ball of the foot in a circular motion to kick an opponent. What seems a fairly easy kick is, in fact, quite complicated, which is why the kick is not normally taught until students have reached about green belt level. As with yoko geri kekomi (side thrust kick), the supporting leg plays an important part and must pivot during the kicking action.

Mawashi Geri from a Static Position

Commence by practising mawashi geri from heiko dachi (parallel stance), concentrating on developing correct leg movement (Figs 300–304).

Step 1

Assume the heiko dachi position with both hands out to the side of the body.

Step 2

The kick is going to be executed at a target directly to the front. Start by bringing the

Fig 300 Step 1

kicking leg up to the side, ensuring that the foot remains lower than the knee, and that the knee of the kicking leg remains behind the line of the hips at this stage. The toes of the kicking foot must be pulled back, exposing the foot, in preparation for making contact with the target. It is important that the back is kept as upright as possible, avoiding the temptation to lean to one side.

Step 3

In a circular movement, rotate the hips towards the target. Simultaneously, pivot the supporting leg so the foot is pointing to the side at the end of the kick. Use the ball of the foot as the striking point.

Step 4

Mawashi geri is a snap kick, and the foot should return quickly to the side and then back to heiko dachi.

Throughout the kick try to maintain good balance on the supporting leg. This may be assisted by keeping the supporting leg slightly bent at the knee throughout the duration of the kick.

Steps 1 to 4 above should then be repeated using the other leg, so that both sides of the body are equally developed.

Fig 301 Step 2

Fig 302 Step 3 (a)

159

Fig 303 Step 3 (b)

Fig 304 Step 4

Stepping Forward

The next step is to practise the kick from zenkutsu dachi (front stance) (Figs 305–311).

STEP 1

Assume the zenkutsu dachi position with both hands at the side.

STEP 2

Pull the rear leg up to the side, ensuring that the foot remains lower than the knee at this point and the knee remains behind the line of the hips. Maintain an upright body position.

STEP 3

In a circular movement, start to move the

Fig 305 Step 1

Fig 306 Step 2 – front view

knee of the kicking leg around to the front, remembering to pivot the supporting foot to a position of 90 degrees.

STEP 4
Continue to kick around to the front using the ball of the foot as the striking point. Roll the right hip over so the foot hits the intended target while parallel to the floor.

STEP 5
Immediately snap the kicking foot back.

STEP 6
Finally, step forward into front stance, ensuring the foot lands so that the feet end up hip-width apart in a strong front stance.

This kicking action can then be performed on the opposite side using the left leg.

Fig 307 Step 2 – side view

Fig 308 Step 3

Mawashi Geri – Variation

The mawashi geri described above is the traditional method of performing this kick. Some instructors teach a slightly different variation in which the knee of the kicking leg travels through the centre to the front, as opposed to the circular action to the side already described.

Common Mistakes

When using mawashi geri, keep the back as upright as possible and keep looking at the target at all times. A common mistake is to lean over too far to the side, which can also result in the eyes being taken off the target.

In performing the traditional mawashi geri, ensure that the knee of the kicking leg moves correctly to the side. At this intermediate position, the knee must remain behind the

Fig 309 Step 4

Fig 310 Step 5

line of the hips, and the foot lower than the knee.

In the photograph (Fig 312), the correct knee and foot position is demonstrated at the intermediate stage. The knee is positioned level with the hips, and the foot below the knee. Note that the body is kept upright.

The next photograph (Fig 313) demonstrates an incorrect knee position, one of the more frequent mistakes. The knee has moved beyond the line of the hip and the foot is raised so that it is level and almost higher than the knee. On this occasion, the body is leaning over to the side.

From the intermediate position, the kick should rotate to the front in a circular movement and, on impact, the foot should be parallel to the ground. This is often the point where the kicking action goes wrong in one of two ways. The foot of the kicking leg either

Fig 311 Step 6

Fig 312 Correct knee position

impacts in an upward or downward direction, resulting in a loss of power. To prevent this happening, try to focus the kick so that it penetrates into the target.

The photograph (Fig 314) demonstrates the position of the foot of the supporting leg. It has pivoted around to the side, allowing the kicking leg to follow the circular movement without strain on the hips or the knee of the supporting leg.

Ushiro Geri (Back Kick)

Ushiro geri can be used for kicking an attacker approaching from behind. However, this is not its only application. Ushiro geri can also be used to kick in different directions by turning the body so that the back faces the direction in which the kick is to go. Whatever the direction of the kick, the method of delivery is the same and the shape of the kick should not alter.

Fig 313 Incorrect knee position

Fig 314 Correct kicking action

This particular kick was developed to attack targets to the rear: it is the advent of competition karate that has resulted in the use of ushiro geri to attack to the front. Generally speaking, it is not advisable to turn your back on an attacker unless circumstances dictate that this is the only option available.

Ushiro Geri from a Static Position

The preparatory moves for ushiro geri are similar to those employed for mae geri (front kick) (Figs 315–321).

STEP 1

Assume the heiko dachi (parallel stance) position with both hands out to the side of the body.

165

Fig 315 Step 1 – front view

Fig 316 Step 1 – side view

STEP 2
Bring the knee of the kicking leg up in front of the body, but ensure that the foot remains parallel to the ground.

STEP 3
Thrust the kicking leg backward in a straight line so that it straightens at the knee, and use the heel of the foot as the point of contact

with the target. The toes of the kicking foot must be pointing downward.

STEP 4
Return the kicking leg to the front before stepping back down into heiko dachi.

Repeat the kick on the other side so that both legs are used equally.

Fig 317 Step 2 – front view

Fig 318 Step 2 – side view

Fig 319 Step 3 – side view

Fig 320 Step 3 – rear view

Fig 321 Step 4

Fig 322 Step 1

IMPORTANT

Ushiro geri is a thrust kick. Concentrate on locking the leg at the end of the kick to maximize power.

Kicking to the Front

The next stage is to practise ushiro geri from zenkutsu dachi (front stance), rotating the hips so that the kick is used to attack a target to the front (Figs 322–327).

STEP 1

Commence in left zenkutsu dachi with the hands positioned at the side.

STEP 2

Rotate the hips to the right (the direction the heel of the rear foot is pointing). Keep looking over the left shoulder at this stage.

STEP 3

Raise the right foot and turn the head to look over the opposite shoulder.

STEP 4

Thrust the kicking leg in a straight line to the rear, using the heel of the foot as the striking surface.

Fig 323 Step 2

Fig 324 Step 3

Fig 325 Step 4

Fig 326 Step 5 (a)

Fig 327 Step 5 (b)

Fig 328 Incorrect

Step 5

Retract the kicking leg and continue to rotate the hips to the right, stepping in the direction of the kick into right zenkutsu dachi.

Common Mistakes

The most common mistake with this kick is that practitioners allow the hip of the kicking leg to rise as the foot is thrust backward. This results in the foot turning to make contact sideways-on. This then becomes yoko geri kekomi (side thrust kick), delivered to the rear. The photograph (Fig 328) demon-strates the result of the left hip being allowed to rise when performing ushiro geri. The foot has turned up and is sideways-on at the point of impact. This can be prevented by con-centrating on keeping the hips square to the ground as the kicking leg is driven backward.

A further common mistake with ushiro geri is failure to kick in a straight line, the kicking leg being allowed to follow a slightly circular route to the target. This is more prevalent in the spinning version. The photograph (Fig 329) demonstrates how this can be avoided by ensuring that the correct knee position is reached at the intermediate stage

Mikazuki geri often features in the karate kata, commencing with heian godan. When this kick is performed well, it can be delivered very quickly. It is frequently used as a feint or preliminary move with finishing techniques following immediately after (Figs 330–334).

STEP 1
Assume the left zenkutsu dachi (front stance) position with both hands out to the side of the body.

Fig 329 Correct

in the kick, and keeping the hips square to the ground as the kicking leg thrusts backward.

Mikazuki Geri (Crescent Kick)

Mikazuki geri is a circular kick using the bottom of the foot to strike an opponent or to block an incoming attack. A variation is to use the ball of the foot as the striking point.

Fig 330 Step 1

171

STEP 2
The kick is going to be executed at a target directly to the front. Commence by bringing the kicking leg up so that the knee is pointing out at an angle of 45 degrees. It is important that the back is kept as upright as possible, avoiding the temptation to lean to one side or backward.

STEP 3
Continue to rotate the kicking foot in an arc towards the target, using the sole of the foot as the striking point.

Fig 332 Step 3

STEP 4
Having executed the kick, step forward and place the foot on the floor in right zenkutsu dachi.

Repeat using the opposite leg to perform the kick again, stepping forward on completion.

Fig 331 Step 2

Fig 333 Step 4 (a)

Gyaku Mawashi Geri (Inside Roundhouse Kick)

Gyaku mawashi geri is a circular kick that follows an arc across the front of the body and out to the side. At first sight, the kick appears weak and awkward. However, it can be very effective if delivered fast, in a snapping action. Good target areas are the stomach, groin, and legs, although with good flexibility the facial area can also be reached (Figs 335–339).

STEP 1
Assume the left zenkutsu dachi (front stance) position with both hands out to the side of the body.

Fig 334 Step 4 (b)

Fig 335 Step 1

Fig 336 Step 2   Fig 337 Step 3

STEP 2

The kick is going to be executed at a target directly to the front. Commence by bringing the kicking leg up so that the knee is pointing across the front of the body at an angle of approximately 45 degrees.

STEP 3

Snap the foot out, pivoting at the knee. The striking surface should be the ball of the foot.

STEP 4

This is a snap kick, so quickly return the foot to the position described at Step 2 following completion of the kick. Return the foot to the ground by stepping forward into right zenkutsu dachi.

Fig 338 Step 4 (a)

Fig 339 Step 4 (b)

Ushiro Mawashi Geri (Reverse Roundhouse Kick)

Ushiro mawashi geri is a circular kick, the reverse of mawashi geri. The kick uses the heel of the foot to make contact with the target and can have surprising results when performed correctly. It is, however, a very advanced kick and often difficult to master.

For safety reasons, when sparring with a partner in freestyle or in competition work, contact with the sole of the foot in place of the heel is usually required.

Start by practising ushiro mawashi geri from zenkutsu dachi (front stance), concentrating on the development of correct leg movement and stability. The initial stages of the kick are similar to ushiro geri (back kick), where it is necessary to spin using the hips so that the back is turned for a split second towards the intended target (Figs 340–344).

STEP 1
Assume the left zenkutsu dachi position with both hands out to the side of the body.

STEP 2
Rotate the hips to the right (the direction the heel of the rear foot is pointing). Keep looking over the left shoulder at this stage.

Fig 341 Step 2

Fig 340 Step 1

STEP 3
Raise the kicking leg up to the side, ensuring that the foot remains lower than the knee, and that the knee remains in line with the hips.

STEP 4
Pivoting at the knee, the foot of the kicking leg should then rotate in a circular, reverse movement towards the target, using the heel

Fig 342 Step 3

Fig 343 Step 4

Fig 344 Step 5

of the foot as the striking point. The kick is a hooking action, and the kicking foot should be withdrawn to the side immediately after completion.

STEP 5

Rotating the hips around to the right, complete the action by stepping down with the kicking leg into right zenkutsu dachi.

During the kick, try and maintain balance on the supporting leg. This may be assisted by keeping the supporting leg slightly bent at the knee throughout the duration of the kick.

Steps 1 to 5 should then be repeated using the other leg so that both sides of the body are equally developed.

Kakato Geri (Axe Kick)

Kakato geri is a kick that strikes in a downward direction, similar to the chopping action of an axe. The target area is usually the top of the head or the back. The kick can also be used to strike an attacker who is on the floor.

To perform the kick it is necessary to swing the leg up high into the air and then down, striking with the heel of the foot. In order to get the kicking leg up to the front, a small circular movement is required. The leg can follow a route from either outside to inside, or the reverse (Fig 345).

Ashi Barai (Sweeping Kick)

Ashi barai is used as a sweeping kick with the intention of knocking down or unbalancing an opponent. It is a fast kick and often used

Fig 345 Kakato geri

Fig 346 Ashi barai

to good effect in competitions or freestyle application. The kick can use either the bottom or the side of the foot, which is targeted towards the opponent's leg. As well as being a sweep, ashi barai can be used as an effective strike to the knee, attacking from either the side or back (Fig 346).

Fumikomi (Stamping Kick)

Fumikomi is used to stamp down on an opponent. It is generally used to strike at the knee, leg and hip areas but does have other applications such as attacking an opponent on the floor.

In order to strike downward, the kicking leg needs to be raised up so that the knee is pulled in towards the chest. From this position, drop downward or kick outward on to the side of the knee or other target area (Fig 347).

Fig 347 Fumikomi

Fig 348 Hiza geri

Fig 349 Hiza geri from the side

Hiza Geri (Knee Kick)

The knee can be used effectively to strike an opponent from close range. It is very powerful and can have a devastating effect. The kick can be deployed in two ways.

The first method is to attack in an upward direction into the groin, stomach or head of the opponent. The second method is to strike in a circular movement, similar in action to a mawashi geri (roundhouse kick). The knee strikes around from the side. In both cases, if the foot of the kicking leg is pointed downward, the muscles across the knee will tense up, reducing the risk of injury on impact (Figs 348–349).

9 Developing Flexibility

It is now readily accepted that performance in most sports can be improved through increased flexibility: karate is no different. In fact, due to the very nature of the mechanics of many karate techniques, poor flexibility can actually inhibit correct application. Furthermore, a lack of flexibility can result in greater stress on the joints and muscles, increasing the likelihood of injury during training.

By improving the range of movement in the shoulders, hips and trunk through stretching, it is possible to achieve greater agility, speed of movement and endurance. This, in turn, will enhance performance. Good flexibility will also help preserve energy as the muscles have less work to do in achieving the range of movement being undertaken.

When devising a training programme for flexibility, it must be remembered that everyone is different, and that the range of movement at a joint can vary considerably from one person to the next. Some people are naturally more flexible than others, and training should be focused according to individual capabilities.

What is Meant by Flexibility?

Flexibility can best be described as the range of movement at a joint such as the hip or shoulder, or a series of joints such as the spine. The range of movement at these joints can be increased if a regular, structured stretching routine is followed, during which the muscles are stretched and held beyond their normal length.

It is important to understand that improved flexibility cannot be achieved overnight. Noticeable results can only be gained through regular, consistent training.

The Physiology of Stretching

In order to comprehend what takes place when a stretch is applied, the role of the receptors in the muscles and tendons, and the resultant neurophysiological process that takes place need to be understood.

All muscles contain receptors, known as muscle spindles, whose role is to monitor and collect information about the length, and rate of change of length, of the muscle. The tendons, which connect the muscles to the bone, also have their own receptors called Golgi tendon organs, whose role is to collect information about the level of tension

181

in the tendon and its associated muscle.

When a muscle is stretched beyond its normal length, the muscle spindles send a message to the nervous system, which results in a reflex response telling the muscle to tighten up. This is a natural, defensive mechanism coming into play to prevent injury to the muscle from over-stretching.

When the Golgi tendon organs identify that the muscle has been stretched, an opposite reaction occurs. The muscle is told to relax: a built-in safety mechanism. The action of the Golgi tendon organs is secondary to the muscle spindles, following between six and ten seconds afterwards. This is when the body realizes that it can cope with the stretch, and the action of the muscle spindles is overridden. This explains why, after a short while in a static stretch, it is possible to stretch the muscle further. The muscle has been told to relax by its Golgi tendon organ.

This physiological process also explains why ballistic stretching is more stressful on the muscles concerned. The pulsing action involved causes the reflex action in which the muscle tightens up and the Golgi tendon organs never get a chance to initiate the muscle relaxation.

There are three main types of stretching exercise used to increase flexibility static stretching, ballistic stretching and assisted stretching.

Static Stretching

Static stretching involves very little movement once the stretch is in place. The muscle should be stretched beyond its normal length and held in position for a period of between ten seconds and two minutes. Throughout the stretch, it is important to remain relaxed and to breathe normally. This will allow the muscle to stretch to a greater length.

Static stretching has been shown to provide excellent results, and the risk of injury, if applied sensibly, is negligible.

The muscle should feel comfortable when held in position. If there is any pain or a sensation of burning, the pressure should be reduced slightly to relieve the pain but ensuring that the muscle is still held beyond its normal length. Each stretch should be undertaken at least three times.

Once the stretch has been held for a period of time, it is possible to move further into the stretch. This should be repeated two or three times, provided the particular stretch is undertaken for sufficient time.

Ballistic Stretching

Ballistic stretching involves applying a stretch to the muscle and then bouncing or pulsing a number of times to increase the stretch. Care has to be taken with this type of stretching because of the increased risk of injury involved: it should not be undertaken until the body is sufficiently warmed up. This method of stretching is not recommended unless a reasonable degree of flexibility already exists.

Assisted Stretching

Assisted stretching, also known as the PNF technique (proprioceptive neuromuscular facilitation), involves working with a partner and is becoming more and more popular because of the successes that can be achieved. It involves passively moving an arm or leg to the limits of its range of movement and then contracting the muscle isometrically.

This is best described with an example. Using the hamstrings at the back of the leg, the PNF method entails a person lying on the floor and raising a leg up until the stretch sensation is felt (flexed at the hip to at least 90 degrees). The partner then provides resistance by pushing on the back of the leg. The person having the stretch applied then pushes against the resistance, resulting in a contraction of the hamstring muscles that have already been stretched. After about ten to fifteen seconds, the muscle should be relaxed. This should be repeated at least three times with the leg being raised further each time.

Stretching and Children

Care must be taken where children are involved because the bone structure in a child does not fully develop until late teens. Children should be encouraged to undertake gentle flexibility training, but avoid excessive stretching that could result in permanent damage.

Guidelines for Stretching

• The body will respond better if the muscles are warmed-up first and the risk of muscle damage is reduced.
• The muscles should remain relaxed throughout the stretching programme,

which can be assisted by maintaining a normal breathing pattern.
• Progress from major muscle groups and joints to the minor ones.
• The muscles should be stretched beyond their normal range and held for between ten seconds and two minutes. The stretch should be comfortable with no pain experienced.
• Once the muscle being stretched becomes accustomed to the position, the stretching sensation will decline. At this point, the stretch should be applied a little further and again held in position.
• In general, any form of bouncing should be avoided as the risk of injury is increased.

Each karate session will commence with a series of stretching exercises that have been chosen with the specific needs of the karate student in mind. A well-balanced routine is described below, and a regular stretching programme should include as many of these as possible. It is desirable to undertake stretching exercises at least every other day. The muscles being stretched are identified in each exercise and illustrated at the end of this chapter.

Exercises

Neck Stretch – Side to Side
Avoiding any jerking movements, gently turn the head from left to right 10–15 times each way. Follow this by turning the head to one side as far as comfortably possible and hold the stretch for at least 10 seconds. Repeat on the opposite side (Fig 350).

Fig 350

Fig 351

Main muscles stretched: sternocleidomastoid, trapezius.

Neck Stretch Shoulder to Shoulder
Avoiding any jerking movements, gently tilt the head from shoulder to shoulder 10–15 times. The stretch should be felt in both the side of the neck and the shoulder. Follow this by tilting the head to one side as far as comfortably possible, and hold the stretch in place for at least 10 seconds. Repeat on the opposite side (Fig 351).

Main muscles stretched: sternocleidomastoid, trapezius.

Stretch Up
From an upright position, entwine the fingers and stretch up and back so that the stretch is felt across the chest and stomach (Fig 352).

This exercise can be varied by stretching backward at an angle of 45 degrees to both the right and left in turn (Figs 353–354).

Main muscles stretched: anterior deltoid, pectoralis major, rectus abdominus.

184

Fig 352

Fig 353

Side Bends

Commence from an upright position with feet at least shoulder-width apart and hands placed at the side, lightly touching the sides of the legs. From this position, keeping the hips square to the front, lean to one side as far as comfortably possible while simultaneously reaching over the head with the opposite arm. Perform this stretch on both sides, holding in position for at least 10 seconds (Fig 355).

Main muscles stretched: external obliques, latissimus dorsi, tensor fascia latae, vastus lateralis.

Trunk Twists

Commence from an upright position with feet at least shoulder-width apart and knees slightly bent. From this position, gently swing the arms from side to side about 10–15 times on each side.

This can be followed by turning as far as comfortably possible in one direction and holding the position for at least 10 seconds.

185

Fig 354

Fig 356

Fig 355

Repeat on the opposite side (Figs 356–357).

Main muscles stretched: external obliques, latissimus dorsi, rectus abdominis, gluteus maximus.

Touching Toes – Hamstring Stretch

Commence from an upright position with the feet together, ensuring the spine is extended. From this start position, gently bend at the waist and reach down towards the floor, feeling the stretch at the back of the legs.

Fig 357

Fig 358

Maintain a comfortable, stretched position for at least 10 seconds (Figs 358–359).

A less stressful variation of this movement is to commence with the legs bent and touch the floor with the hands. From this position, keep the hands on the floor and straighten the legs as far as comfortably possible.

Main muscles stretched: the hamstring group that consists of three muscles at the back of the upper leg – biceps femoris, semitendinosus, semimembranosus.

Hamstring Stretch – Legs Parted
This variation of the hamstring stretch will also stretch the lower back muscles.

Part the legs to about twice hip-width and keep the legs straight. Bend at the waist, moving the chest towards each knee in turn. Hold the stretch on each side for 10–15 seconds (Figs 360–361).

Main muscles stretched: biceps femoris, semitendinosus, semimembranosus, latissimus dorsi, teres major.

187

Fig 359

Fig 360

Fig 361

While the legs are in the same position, a further stretch can be made to the front by moving the head down between the legs (Fig 362).

Main muscles stretched: biceps femoris, semitendimous, semimembranosus, latissimus dorsi.

Once the body is used to this position, the legs should be parted further and the series of stretches repeated.

Fig 362

on the floor on the inside of the feet. From this position, use the elbows to push the knees out until the stretch can be felt in the inner thigh (Fig 363).

After this position has been held for at least 10 seconds the muscles should have relaxed, enabling the knees to be pushed out a little further. Again, push the knees out and hold for another 10 seconds. Repeat for a third time.

Main muscles stretched: gracilis, pectineus, adductor longus, adductor magnus.

Inner Thigh and Hamstring Stretch

From the kiba dachi positions described above, drop down over the right knee and straighten the left leg. At the same time, pull the left foot back towards the body. Using the elbow, gently push the right knee out to the side so that the stretch is felt in the inner thigh. Hold this position (Fig 364).

Follow this by leaning down with the chest towards the left knee so that the stretch is felt

Inner Thigh Stretch

From kiba dachi (horse riding or straddle leg stance), bend forward and place both hands

Fig 363

Fig 364

Fig 365

the stretch is felt at the inner thigh and groin. Hold this position for at least 10 seconds then extend the legs further apart and hold. Repeat at least three times.

This stretch can be taken a step further by stretching down towards the front and each knee in succession, holding the stretch at each position. When bending, ensure that this is from the waist and keep the spine straight (Fig 366).

Main muscles stretched: pectineus, adductor longus, adductor magnus, adductor brevis, adductor gracilis, biceps femoris, latissimus dorsi, gluteus maximus.

Seated Hamstring Stretch

Sit on the floor with the back straight and the legs together. From this position, gently lean forward until the stretch can be felt at the back of the legs and held comfortably. When the body is used to this position, lean forward a little further and hold once more. Repeat three times.

Main muscles stretched: biceps femoris, semitendimous, semimembranosus.

Depending on the level of flexibility, this stretch can be taken a step further by taking

on the back of the leg. At the same time, keep the pressure on the right knee to prevent it from moving in as the chest goes down (Fig 365).

Main muscles stretched: biceps femoris, semitendimous, semimembranosus, gracilis, pectineus.

Seated Groin Stretch

Sit on the floor with the back upright and the legs outstretched. Pull the feet back so that

Fig 366

Fig 368

Fig 367

and hold again. Carry out this exercise three times and then carefully relax the legs.

Main muscles stretched: pectineus,

hold of the feet and pulling back (Fig 367).

Additional muscles stretched: gastrocnemius, soleus.

Seated groin stretch

A number of exercises can be undertaken from this position. Sit on the floor with the back straight. Bring both feet in to the centre so that the soles of the feet touch (Fig 368).

Commence by moving the knees simultaneously up and down for about 20 seconds. Then, using the elbows, gently push both knees down towards the floor so that the stretch can be felt at the inner thigh. Hold for about 10 seconds, push down a little further,

Fig 369

adductor longus, adductor magnus, adductor brevis, adductor gracilis.

Note: the PNF technique can be used with this variation. When applying downward pressure or resistance with the elbows, push upward with the knees and hold the resultant tension for 10 seconds. Then relax, push the knees down further and repeat. Repeat this exercise three times.

A further stretch from this seated position is to lean forward between the legs, bending from the waist. Again, get into a comfortable position and hold (Fig 369).

Additional muscles stretched: biceps femoris, semitendimous, semimembranosus, latissimus dorsi, gluteus maximus.

Seated Hamstring and Groin Stretch

While seated on the floor, extend the left leg out to the front and pull the right foot up into the groin so that the sole of the right foot touches the inside of the upper left leg. Straighten the spine and lean forward, bending at the waist, until the stretch is felt at both the back of the extended leg and the outside of right hip (Figs 370–371).

Fig 370

Hold the stretch in place for at least 10 seconds. Repeat this exercise three times and, where possible, bend lower with the chest each time.

Main muscles stretched: pectineus, adductor longus, adductor magnus, adductor brevis, gracilis, biceps femoris, semitendimous, semimembranosus, latissimus dorsi, gluteus maximus.

Fig 371

Ankle Exercise

Remaining seated on the floor, take the right foot over the left leg. Rotate the foot at the ankle, changing direction after about 10 seconds (Fig 372).

Main muscles stretched: hallucis longus, digitorum longus, tibialis posterior.

Inner Groin Stretch

While seated on the floor, extend the left leg out to the front and pull the right foot up to the rear. Using the elbow, push the rear knee backward to open up the hip (Fig 373).

Maintain the stretch in a comfortable position for at least 10 seconds. Repeat three times, increasing the length of the stretch each time.

Fig 373

Fig 372

Main muscles stretched: pectineus, adductor longus, adductor magnus, adductor brevis, adductor gracilis.

Outer Thigh Stretch

There are two good exercises for the outer thigh muscles that follow on from each other.

Commence with the left leg outstretched to the front. Cross the left leg with the right foot so that the right foot is flat on the floor at the outside of the left upper leg. Using the left elbow, push the right knee to the left (Fig 374).

The stretch can be increased by simultaneously twisting to the right while keeping the pressure on the left knee.

From this position, bending the left leg at the knee, tuck the left foot back into the buttocks and then lean down towards the

Fig 375

Fig 374

Standing Hip and Thigh Stretch

Stand upright with the feet shoulder-width apart and the knees slightly bent. From this position, raise the knee up to the chest using the hands to assist and hold for at least 10 seconds (Fig 377).

right foot until the stretch is felt on the outside of the right hip (Fig 375).

Main muscles stretched: gluteus maximus, external obliques, rectus abdominus.

Shoulder and Side Stretch

Commence by kneeling on all fours. From this position, reach as far forward as possible with the hands outstretched while sitting back on the heels of the feet. The stretch should be felt in the shoulders, back and sides (Fig 376).

Main muscles stretched: latissimus dorsi, teres major, deltoid.

Fig 376

Fig 377

Fig 378

Fig 379

Fig 380

Fig 381

Fig 382

Main muscle stretched: gluteus maximus.

This stretch may be continued by moving the foot around to the side and holding it in a stretched position (Fig 378).

Additional muscles stretched: pectineus, adductor longus, adductor brevis, adductor gracilis.

Standing Quadriceps Stretch

Stand upright with the feet shoulder-width apart and the knees slightly bent. From this position, raise the foot up behind the body towards the buttocks, using the hands to assist. At the same time, push the hips gently forward to increase the stretch, and hold (Fig 379).

Main muscles stretched: the quadriceps group which consist of four muscles at the front and side of the legs – vastus medialis, vastus intermedius, vastus lateralis, rectus femoris. Additionally, this exercise stretches the lliopsoas muscle.

Fig 383

Shoulder Stretch

Cross the body with the right hand so that it is positioned over the opposite shoulder. With the left hand, gently ease the arm around further until the stretch is felt and can be comfortably held (Fig 380).

Main muscles stretched: trapezius, deltoid.

A variation of this stretch is to pull the elbow backward and down so that the hand is over and behind the right shoulder (Fig 381).

Wrist Exercises

Two good wrist exercises are described below.

Bend the hand at the wrist so that the hand is turned in towards the body (Fig 382).

Main muscles stretched: extensor digitorium, extensor digiti minimi, extensor carpi ulnaris.

The second stretch involves bending the hand at the wrist so that it is palm upward and pushed away from the body (Fig 383).

Main muscles stretched: palmaris longus, · flexor carpi radialis, flexor carpi ulnaris.

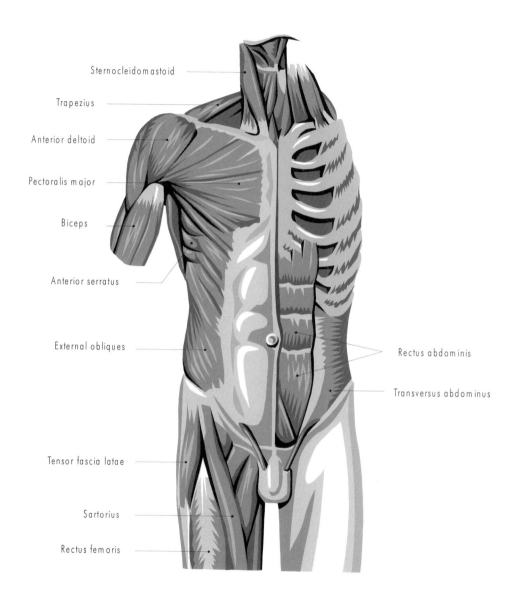

Sternocleidomastoid

Trapezius

Anterior deltoid

Pectoralis major

Biceps

Anterior serratus

External obliques

Rectus abdominis

Transversus abdominus

Tensor fascia latae

Sartorius

Rectus femoris

Fig 384 Muscles of the trunk – front view

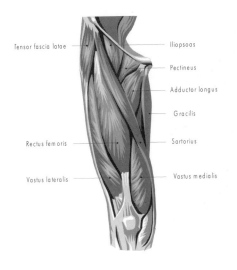

Tensor fascia latae
Iliopsoas
Pectineus
Adductor longus
Gracilis
Rectus femoris
Sartorius
Vastus lateralis
Vastus medialis

Fig 386 Upper leg – front view

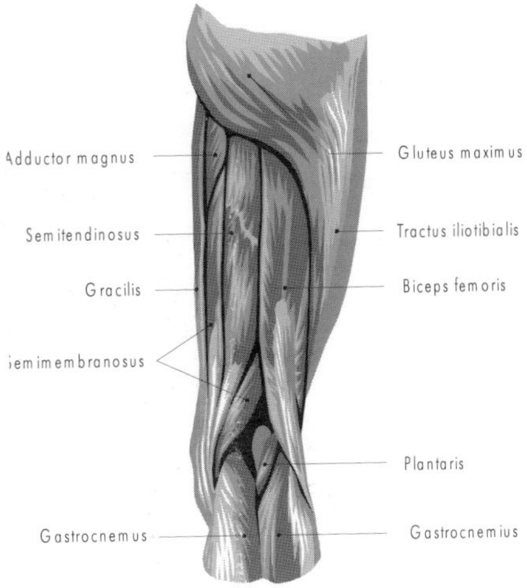

Adductor magnus
Gluteus maximus
Semitendinosus
Tractus iliotibialis
Gracilis
Biceps femoris
Semimembranosus
Plantaris
Gastrocnemus
Gastrocnemius

Fig 387 Upper leg – rear view

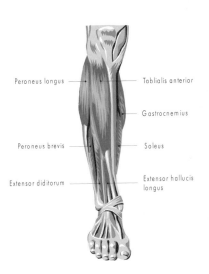

Peroneus longus
Tablialis anterior
Gastrocnemius
Peroneus brevis
Soleus
Extensor diditorum
Extensor hallucis longus

Fig 388 Lower leg – front view

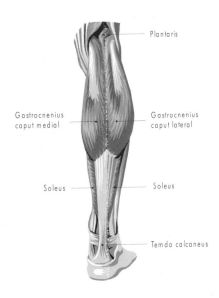

Plantaris
Gastrocnenius caput medial
Gastrocnenius caput lateral
Soleus
Soleus
Temdo calcaneus

Fig 389 Lower leg – rear view

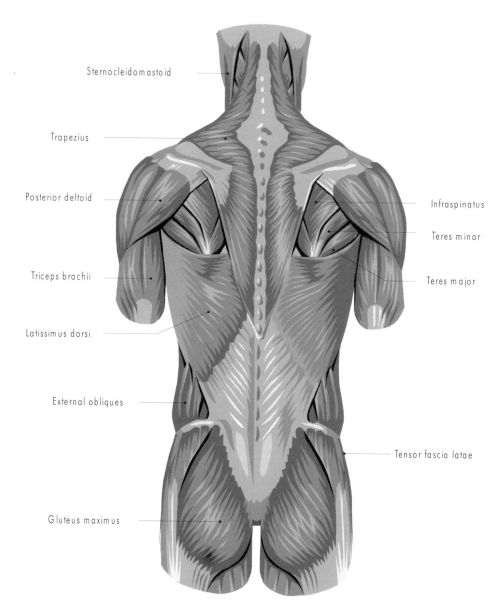

Sternocleidomastoid

Trapezius

Posterior deltoid

Triceps brachii

Latissimus dorsi

External obliques

Gluteus maximus

Infraspinatus

Teres minor

Teres major

Tensor fascia latae

Fig 385 Muscles of the trunk – rear view

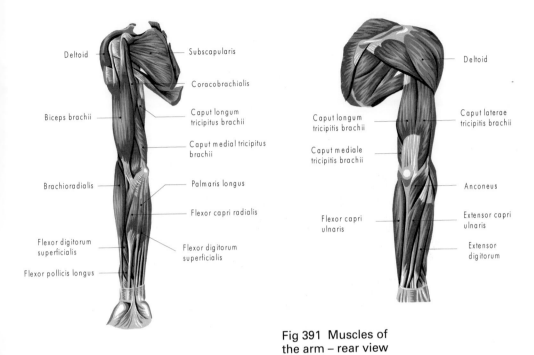

Deltoid

Subscapularis

Coracobrachialis

Biceps brachii

Caput longum
tricipitus brachii

Caput medial tricipitus
brachii

Brachioradialis

Palmaris longus

Flexor capri radialis

Flexor digitorum
superficialis

Flexor digitorum
superficialis

Flexor pollicis longus

Deltoid

Caput longum
tricipitis brachii

Caput laterae
tricipitis brachii

Caput mediale
tricipitis brachii

Anconeus

Flexor capri
ulnaris

Extensor capri
ulnaris

Extensor
digitorum

**Fig 391 Muscles of
the arm – rear view**

**Fig 390 Muscles of
the arm – front view**

10 Target Areas

This chapter is intended for the serious martial artist and contains dangerous techniques. Great care must be taken when striking any of the areas described below, and only then under the supervision of a qualified instructor. Striking either vulnerable points or pressure points must never be undertaken indiscriminately or without understanding the likely outcome and method of resuscitation.

In order to understand the striking points of the body, a distinction has to be made between what are referred to as pressure points and those that can be classed as vulnerable points. A vulnerable point is, as its name implies, a part of the body where it can be considered vulnerable or weak, but is not a pressure point. An example is the nose, which being a sensory organ and full of nerves, offers a good striking point and is vulnerable to attack. Further examples of vulnerable points are the joints, which can be bent and manipulated to cause pain, and even broken to incapacitate.

Pressure points can be defined as gateways into the body through which great pain can be inflicted, and the nervous, respiratory or circulatory systems disrupted or shut down. They are usually identified by their location on acupuncture meridians. An acupuncturist will apply pressure or manipulate the various points for medicinal or therapeutic purposes, whereas the martial artist will strike or apply pressure to injure or debilitate.

The striking of pressure points can vary from the basic striking of single points to the more advanced science of hitting various combinations of points simultaneously, or in series, to increase the resultant effect. Many years of study are required to understand this topic fully, which is almost a discipline in its own right. This section is intended for reference purposes only and is not a substitute for personal instruction.

1. TOP OF THE HEAD – BREGMA
This is the point where the frontal and parietal bones meet. A strike in a downward direction using tetsui uchi (hammer fist strike) may result in unconsciousness and possible brain damage.

2. FOREHEAD
Three points on the gallbladder meridian (GB13, 14 and 15) are located in close proximity at either side of the upper forehead. These points can be struck simultaneously to bring unconsciousness, using techniques

such as teisho uchi (palm heel strike). The three points should be struck inward with a slight glancing action to the side.

3. TEMPLE (SPHENOID BONE)
The temple is structurally weak, being concave in shape, and a strike to this point should only be undertaken in extreme circumstances. Unconsciousness, brain damage and even death may result.

4. NOSE
The nose, being full of nerves, is an effective place to strike. Even a light tap will cause the nose to bleed, and temporary blindness from the watering of the eyes.

5. BETWEEN THE EYES
Located between the eyes, in the centre of the head, is one of the more dangerous striking points. The strike should be in an upward direction, which will cause disorientation and unconsciousness, even death.

6. CHEEKBONES
A point located on the small intestine meridian (SI18) is situated under the cheek-bone in the centre of the face. This provides a good striking point in an upward direction towards the centre of the head. A strike to this point can result in unconsciousness.

7. BEHIND THE EAR
This is one of the more effective striking points but often difficult to get access to. It is situated on the triple warmer meridian (TW17), located behind the ear lobe. The angle of strike can be either in an upward direction towards the centre of the skull, or

from back to front. A strike to this point could prove fatal.

8. MANDIBLE (LOWER JAW BONE)
The mandible is the only moveable bone in the head, and a strike can dislocate the jaw. Also located on the cheekbone is a point on the stomach meridian (ST5) that provides a good striking point. This point can be struck inward and towards the back of the head, or inward in a forward direction towards the chin. A good knock-out point.

9. NECK
The whole of the neck area provides a good target but must be selected with care. The jugular vein and carotid artery run along the side of the neck, and a blow to this area could rupture or damage either of them, which could result in death. There are also four acupuncture points located on the neck in the region below the mandible (lower jaw bone): two on the large intestine meridian (LI17 and 18), and two on the stomach meridian (ST9 and 10).

10. THROAT
The throat may be divided into two distinct striking areas. First, there is the jugular notch, located in the centre of the throat below the Adam's apple but above the manubrium bone (top of sternum). This is a soft area where the trachea is exposed and unprotected. A slight jab to this point will cause an uncomfortable sensation, while a more powerful strike could prove fatal. The second area of the throat is the thyroid carti-lage. In men, this area is prominent and easily identifiable by the Adam's apple.

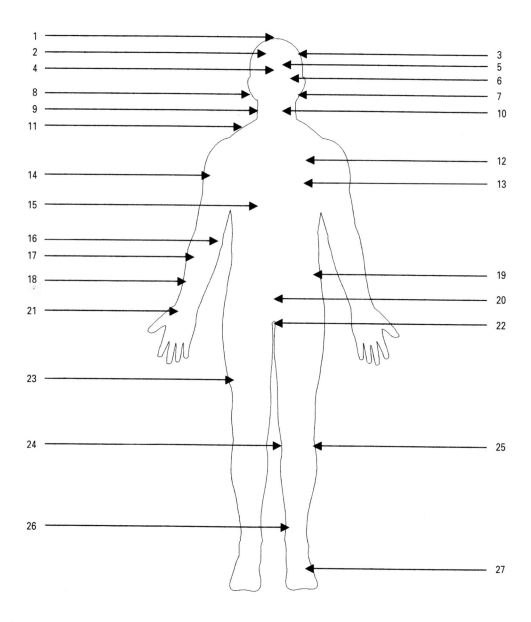

Fig 392 Target areas of the front

Even a light strike to this point could prove fatal.

11. BRAXIAL PLEXUS

The brachial plexus extends from the lower part of the side of the neck across the shoulders. It is the union of a number of nerves and provides an effective striking point. A good strike to this area will impair the use of the arms.

12. CHEST ABOVE THE NIPPLE

The stomach meridian runs in a straight line down from the shoulder to the nipple, and a number of points are located in close proximity along this line (ST13, 14 and 15). The angle of strike should be in and slightly downward. A relatively hard strike can cause nausea.

13. CHEST BELOW THE NIPPLE

A pressure point on the spleen meridian (SP17) is located approximately 2.5cm (1in) below and 2.5cm (1in) to the outside of the nipple. A strike to this point, angled from the outside in towards the centre of the body, will cause severe pain and weaken the opponent.

14. TOP OF THE BICEPS

A point that can be struck to good effect on the upper arm is located at the top of the biceps on the lung meridian (L2). A strike to this point will deaden the arm.

15. XIPHOID PROCESS/SOLAR PLEXUS

The xiphoid process is a strip of cartilage located at the lower end of the sternum, and the solar plexus is situated immediately below. It is difficult to develop muscle over these areas, making them good gateways into the body. A light strike to this region will wind the person; a powerful blow could result in unconsciousness and damage to the heart.

16. INSIDE OF THE UPPER ARM

One of the more effective striking points on the arm is located on the inside of the upper arm, approximately 2.5cm (1in) above the elbow, at the base of the biceps. This is located on the heart meridian (H2). A strike to this point will severely weaken the arm.

17. INSIDE OF THE FOREARM

Located on the thumb side of the inner forearm, approximately 2.5cm (1in) down from the crease of the elbow, is a point located on the lung meridian (L5). This point is often accessible to strike and manipulate in grappling applications.

18. CENTRE FOREARM

This point is located on the thumb side of the forearm at the edge of the bone, at approximately the centre of the lower arm. This is an effective place to attack the arms during blocking applications and, when struck, will feel like an electric shock shooting down the arm. This again is an acupuncture point on the lung meridian (L6). The angle of strike should be in and down, towards the wrist.

19. BELOW THE FLOATING RIBS

One of the more effective striking areas of the lower abdomen is located immediately below the floating ribs on both sides of the body. In acupuncture, this is on the liver meridian (LIV13). The direction of strike should be in a straight line, or in towards the centre and

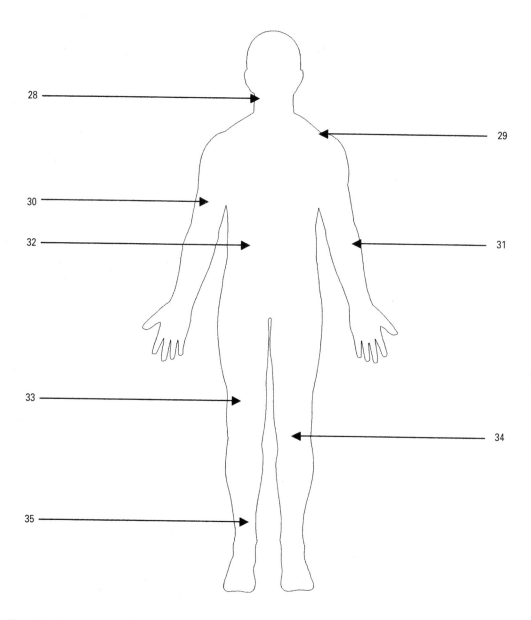

28

29

30

32

31

33

34

35

Fig 393 Target areas of the back

slightly upward. This is a dangerous point to strike as it can cause damage to the spleen.

20. BELOW THE NAVEL
Located in the centre of the body below the navel are a number of points on the conception vessel meridian (CV5, 6 and 7). The strike should be directed downward.

21. WRIST POINTS
The wrist has a number of pressure points, located on the back and front, which should be studied. Although these can be struck, they are more often used in wrist grabs prior to striking other points.

22. TESTICLES
The testicles provide an obvious striking point on men, but care must be taken as this area is not always accessible.

23. OUTSIDE OF THE UPPER LEG
A point located halfway down the outside of the upper leg is the traditional striking point used to cause the 'dead leg' effect. There are two acupuncture points located here on the gallbladder meridian (GB31 and 32). A strike to either point, ideally directed in from the side, will cause extreme pain and incapacitate the leg for some time.

24. INSIDE LEG ABOVE THE KNEE
A strike to this point, which is on the spleen meridian (SP10), is extremely painful and causes the leg to buckle. A disadvantage, however, is that it is not always accessible.

25. KNEE
The knee provides a good striking area, as major damage can be caused to the leg at this point, resulting in incapacitation. Depending on circumstances, the knee joint can be struck from the front, back or sides.

26. INSIDE LOWER LEG
Three acupuncture points are located in close proximity on the inside of the lower leg, approximately 10cm (4in) above the ankle. These comprise two on the kidney meridian (K7 and 8), and one on the spleen meridian (SP6).

27. FOOT
There are a number of pressure points located on the foot but it is not necessary to worry too much about their exact location. A stamp to any part of the top of the foot will cause extreme pain.

28. BACK OF THE NECK
This is one of the regularly used target areas because of its ready accessibility. The pressure point is situated on the gallbladder meridian (GB20), and is located adjacent to the spine, slightly below the line of the skull. As with most acupuncture points, this is bilateral (located on both sides of the body). The strike should be directed in and up towards the centre of the head. A light strike to this point will daze or stun the opponent, while a more powerful blow will cause unconsciousness and possible brain damage.

29. BACK OF THE SHOULDER
This point is on the gallbladder meridian (GB21), located approximately 2.5cm (1in) below the shoulder, at the mid-point

between the spine and the upper arm. A strike to this point will cause intense pain and, dependent on the power used, even unconsciousness.

30. UPPER ARM

The triple warmer (three-heater) meridian runs along the centre of the triceps on the back of the upper arm. Two points on the triceps are of particular interest. Situated directly in the centre of the muscle is a point (TW11). When struck, it deadens the arm and can knock the person to the ground. A classic application is to use gedan barai (downward block) to strike this point. The second point (TW12) is located approximately 2.5cm (1in) above the elbow. This point should be rubbed rather than struck, as this causes the arm muscles to relax involuntarily and weaken. The application of pressure should be in a sawing action across the point and slightly down towards the elbow.

31. BACK OF THE FOREARM

A strike to the back of the forearm at a point on the large intestine (colon) meridian (LI10) will deaden the arm. The point is located approximately 2.5cm (1in) from the crease of the elbow, on the thumb side of the back of the forearm.

32. KIDNEYS

The kidneys provide a good but dangerous target area. They are located on both sides of the body, immediately below the ribs. Even a light strike can cause haemorrhage and shock, while a more powerful blow can result in death.

33. BACK OF THE LEG

This point is on the bladder meridian (B51), located in the centre of the back of the upper leg. A powerful kick or strike to this region will deaden the leg and cause some pain.

34. BACK OF THE KNEE

A kick or strike to the back of the knee can cause severe joint damage, resulting in incapacitation. There are four accessible pressure points just above the crease of the knee: three on the bladder meridian (B52, 53 and 54), and one on the kidney meridian (K10).

35. BASE OF THE CALF

A pressure point on the bladder meridian is located in the centre of the leg, at the base of the calf muscle. In addition to inflicting pain, a kick or strike to this point will cause the leg to collapse.

Conclusion

As stated at the start of this chapter, the target areas discussed are intended for reference purposes only, and great care must be taken when striking any of the points described.

From a martial perspective, it is essential that target areas are visualized at all times, whether performing kata, kumite or basic techniques. Never just go through the motions of performing a technique, concentrate instead on the purpose of the movement being undertaken.

11 The Law and Self-Defence

'Karate ni sente nashi'
(There is no first attack in karate)

'Karate ni sente nashi' is a well-known karate saying which is often associated with Sensei Gichin Funakoshi, and is the inscription on his tombstone. However, it is now apparent that it goes back to well before his time. Patrick McCarthy's translation of Shoshin Nagamine's *Tales of Okinawa's Great Masters* attributes the saying to a famous Zen prelate named Muso Soseki (1275–1351). Putting its origins to one side, it is a principle that is known to have permeated Okinawan karate for centuries. Clearly, it is a profound statement, but the passage of time has obscured its original meaning, which must now be a matter of personal interpretation. At first sight, the principle of no first attack presents the martial artist with a dilemma, as it conflicts with the concept of employing a pre-emptive strike in self-defence. So where does one stand?

The decision as to how much force may be used in self-defence can only be made at the time, and will be dependent on a number of different factors. What must be considered is that, at some point in the future, the actions may be brought under close scrutiny and justification required. This is especially true in the case of martial artists who, in the eyes of the law, are all considered experts. In making any such decision, it is important to be aware of the legal situation and what protection it affords. To this end, the main purpose of this chapter is to provide a basic understanding of these provisions as far as they apply to self-defence.

Karate techniques can be very effective in self-defence. When under attack or confronted with potential physical violence, personal survival will be the prime objective of any use of force. The use of force in self-defence is covered by statutory and common law, both of which allow for what is referred to as 'reasonable force' to be applied against an attacker.

The statutory element is contained within Section 3 of the Criminal Law Act 1967, which provides that a person may use 'such force as is reasonable in the circumstances in the prevention of crime'. The section also includes the use of such force in effecting or assisting in the lawful arrest of offenders, or persons unlawfully at large. Therefore, by virtue of the fact that the force is invariably being used to prevent the continuance of a crime, this part of the law allows for reasonable force to be used in self-defence, defence of another person or defence of property.

However, the key word is 'reasonable'. What does this mean? What is 'such force as is reasonable in the circumstances'? This is where the common law element should be examined. In a case[1] that was heard before the Court of Appeal as long ago as 1909, it was said: 'When the issue of self-defence is raised, it is an important consideration that the person defending himself should have demonstrated by his actions that he did not want to fight. He must show he was prepared to temporize and disengage and perhaps make some physical withdrawal'.

In another case[2] that was heard before the Court of Appeal, this time in 1971, the presiding judge made the following statement, which indicates the current legal opinion on the use of force in self-defence: 'It is both good law and good sense that a man who is attacked may defend himself but may only do what is reasonably necessary'.

These two cases serve to reinforce the principle that the use of force as a means of self-defence is acceptable, provided the force used is reasonable and only used in self-defence. Once the threat of assault has subsided, so must the force used. It would not be acceptable, having overpowered the assailant, to become the aggressor.

[1] Regina v. Deanna
[2] Regina v. Palmer

Weapons

If a person is entitled to use reasonable force in self-defence, it follows that when a person is attacked, he may use anything available to defend himself, within the bounds of what is reasonable. However, a clear distinction must be made between the legality of using an article that happens to be available at the time of an attack, and carrying the article for purposes of self-defence.

The Prevention of Crime Act 1953, Section 1, states: 'Any person who without lawful authority or reasonable excuse, the proof of which shall lie on him, has with him in any public place any offensive weapon shall be guilty of an offence'. This is the primary legislation covering the carrying of such weapons. It clearly prohibits the carrying of weapons in public places under normal circumstances.

An 'offensive weapon' is defined as any article made, or adapted for use, to cause injury to another person, or intended by the person having it with him for such use. However, the definition requires further examination.

The first part deals with offensive weapons *per se*, where there is little doubt as to their intended purpose: items designed specifically to cause injury, such as flick knives or knuckle dusters; or items that have been deliberately adapted for the purpose, such as a metal comb, sharpened along one edge.

The second part of the definition deals with articles which, although are not offensive weapons in themselves, are intended to cause injury by the person carrying them. This, therefore, requires a specific state of mind and extends the offence to cover everyday items being carried for purposes of self-defence, such as a screwdriver. A person carrying a screwdriver under normal circumstances does not commit an offence. However, if it is being carried for defensive purposes in the event of attack, it can then be argued that it is an article intended to cause injury, and the offence is committed.

It is hoped that the above summary of the law helps answer some of the questions that arise in this difficult area.

In conclusion, consider again the saying 'karate ni sente nashi' which opened this chapter. There is a school of thought, which is probably closely aligned to its intended meaning, that it stands for the fundamental principle that a martial artist should never be the aggressor but remain calm and controlled, only using the fighting skills when absolutely essential. Sensei Gichin Funakoshi wrote in *Karate-do Kyohan* that 'to become the object of an attack is an indication that there was an opening in one's guard, and the important thing is to be on guard at all times'. It was also his view that when all avenues of escape have closed, and the need to defend oneself arises, then such defence must not be half-hearted. One should attack 'using maximum strength in one blow to a vital point'. This principle is contained in the maxim 'ikken hissatsu', which translates as 'kill with one blow'.

It can be seen, therefore, that there is no conflict between 'karate ni sente nashi' and employing a pre-emptive strike in self-defence, as long as such a course of action is justified and reasonable in the circumstances.

12 Conclusion

Shotokan Karate was always intended to be a reference book, which could be consulted at any stage of training. I hope it has proved useful both as a practical guide for those in the early years of training, and to enhance the knowledge of all karateka, regardless of grade. If I have achieved this, then I go away satisfied that I have given something back to karate in return for the years of pleasure I have derived from my study of this truly intriguing and fascinating art.

Remember that karate is a lifelong study, not to be rushed. You will often find that just as you think you are approaching your destination, you will turn the corner to find another long road ahead, with no end in sight. Whatever the stage of your journey, I implore you to open your mind to wider horizons and take in the scenery. To this end, never turn down an opportunity to train with different martial art instructors, regardless of style. Each will have something to offer.

There is no such thing as the 'best' type of martial art, each has its own strengths and weaknesses. Tap into others and draw on their strengths. Then, with diligent study, correct focus, and hard work, you will become a more complete martial artist.

Sun Tzu, a famous Chinese military strategist, who lived in the fifth century BC, wrote in his text *The Art of War*, 'know your enemy like yourself and a hundred battles you enter, a hundred battle you will emerge victorious'. I leave you with these parting thoughts. How many of us really know ourselves, our own strengths, weaknesses and limitations? Furthermore, how many of us are willing to admit to them?

Remember the first line of the Dojo Kun:

Hitotsu! Jinkaku Kansei ni tsutomuru koto.

(One! to strive for the perfection of character.)

Terminology

The Japanese have heavily influenced karate in recent times and a number of their customs permeate traditional karate styles. Techniques will often be referred to by their Japanese names and the commands used within the dojo will be in that language. This can be quite confusing for people in the early stages of karate training.

As a guide, the most commonly used Japanese names and commands are listed below. Although comprehensive, the list is not exhaustive and is intended as a point of reference only.

Karateka preparing for senior grades will be expected to have a good working knowledge of Japanese terminology, and some associations include an oral examination within the Dan grading syllabus.

For ease of reference, the names are first provided under relevant categories and then within an alphabetical list.

Commands

Hajime	Start/begin
Kamaete	Go into position
Kiritsu	Stand up/rise
Mawate	Turn
Otagai ni rei	Bow to each other
Seiza	Sit straight
Sensei ni rei	Bow to the sensei
Shomen ni rei	Bow to the front
Yame	Stop
Yoi	Prepare/get ready

Dachi (Stances)

Dachi	Stance
Fudo dachi	Rooted stance
Hachiji dachi	Open leg stance
Heiko dachi	Parallel stance
Heisoku dachi	Informal attention stance
Hengetsu dachi	Half-moon stance
Jiyu ippon kumite	Semi-freestyle sparring stance
Jiyu kumite gamae	Freestyle stance
Kiba dachi	Horse riding/straddle leg stance
Kokutsu dachi	Back stance
Kosa dachi	Cross-legged stance
Musubi dachi	Informal attention stance
Neko ashi dachi	Cat stance
Renoji dachi	L-stance
Sanchin dachi	Hour-glass stance
Shiko dachi	Square stance
Shizentai	Natural position

Sochin dachi	Strong/calm stance
Teiji dachi	T-stance
Zenkutsu dachi	Front stance

Zuki (Punching)

Age zuki	Rising punch
Awase zuki	Two-armed combination punch
Choku zuki	Straight punch
Gyaku zuki	Reverse punch
Jun zuki	Following punch
Kage zuki	Hook punch
Kara zuki	Empty punch
Kizami zuki	Jabbing punch
Mawashi zuki	Roundhouse punch
Morote zuki	Double fist punch
Oi zuki	Stepping punch
Sanbon zuki	Three level punches
Sokumen zuki	Side punch
Tate zuki	Vertical punch
Ura zuki	Close punch
Yama zuki	U-punch/mountain punch
Yumi zuki	Bow punch
Zuki	Punch

Uchi (Striking)

Age empi uchi	Rising/upper elbow strike
Atoshi empi uchi	Downward elbow strike
Empi uchi	Elbow strike
Haito uchi	Ridge hand strike
Haiwan uchi	Back of the arm strike
Hiraken uchi	Fore knuckle strike
Ippon ken uchi	One knuckle strike
Kakuto uchi	Crane head strike

Keito uchi	Chicken head wrist strike
Kizami zuki	Jabbing punch
Mawashi empi uchi	Roundhouse elbow strike
Nakadaka ken uchi	Middle finger strike
Nihon nukite	Two finger strike
Nukite uchi	Spear hand strike
Shihon nukite	Four finger spear hand strike
Shuto uchi	Knife hand strike
Teisho uchi	Palm heel strike
Tettsui uchi	Bottom fist strike
Uchi	Strike
Uchi waza	Striking techniques
Uraken uchi	Back fist strike
Ushiro empi uchi	Reverse/back elbow strike
Yoko empi uchi	Side elbow strike

Uke (Blocking)

Age uke	Upper rising block
Awase uke	Combination block
Gedan barai	Downward block
Haishu uke	Back of hand block
Haiwan uke	Back arm block
Juji uke	X-block
Kakiwake uke	Wedge/push aside block
Keito uke	Chicken head block
Kosa uke	Crossing block
Manji uke	Vortex block
Morote uke	Augmented block
Nagashi uke	Sweeping block
Osae uke	Pressing block
Otoshi uke	Dropping block
Shuto uke	Knife hand block
Soto ude uke	Outside forearm block

Sukui uke	Scooping block
Tate shuto uke	Vertical knife hand block
Teisho uke	Palm heel block
Tekubi kake uke	Wrist hooking block
Uchi ude uke	Inside forearm block
Uke	Block

Geri (Kicking)

Ashi barai	Sweeping kick
Fumikiri	Cutting kick
Fumikomi	Stamping kick
Gedan kesage	Lower level downward kick
Geri	Kick
Gyaku mawashi geri	Inside roundhouse kick
Hiza geri	Knee kick
Kakato geri	Axe kick
Keage	Snap
Kekomi	Thrust
Mae geri	Front kick
Mae geri keage	Front snap kick
Mae geri kekomi	Front thrust kick
Mae tobi geri	Front jumping kick
Mawashi geri	Roundhouse kick
Mikazuki geri	Crescent kick
Nami ashi	Returning wave kick
Ren geri	Combination kicking
Tobi geri	Jumping kick
Ushiro geri	Back kick
Ushiro mawashi geri	Reverse roundhouse kick
Yoko geri	Side kick
Yoko geri keage	Side snap kick
Yoko geri kekomi	Side thrust kick
Yoko tobi geri	Side jumping kick

Parts of the Body

Gaiwan	Outside of the forearm
Haishu	Back of the hand
Haisoku	Instep
Haiwan	Back of the forearm
Kakato	Heel
Koshi	Ball of the foot
Naiwan	Inside of the forearm
Shuwan	Underside of the forearm
Sokutei	Sole of the foot
Sokuto	Edge of the foot
Te	Hand
Tekubi	Wrist
Tsumasaki	Tip of the toes
Wan	Arm

Miscellaneous

Ashi sabaki	Leg movement
Bunkai	Application/analysis of kata
Dan	Rank/level (master grade)
Deshi	Student
Do	Way
Dogi	Karate uniform
Dojo	Way/place
Gohon kumite	Five-step sparring
Hanmi	Half body stance (hips facing sideways)
Hara	Centre of the abdomen
Hidari	Left
Hikite	Withdrawing hand
Ippon	One

Jiyu ippon kumite	Semi-freestyle sparring
Kaeshi ippon kumite	Returning one-step sparring
Kan	Hall
Kara	Empty
Karate-do	Way of the empty hand
Karateka	Person that practises karate-do
Kata	Pre-arranged formal exercise (forms)
Kiai	Loud shout to demonstrate martial spirit
Kihon	Basics
Kihon ippon kumite	One-step sparring
Kokyu	Breathing
Kumite	Sparring
Kyu	Rank/grade
Kyusho	Vital points
Maai	Distancing
Mae	Front
Makiwara	Striking board
Migi	Right
Okuri jiyu ippon	Sparring with two attacks
Sanbon kumite	Three-step sparring
Sempai	One's senior
Sensei	Instructor/master
Shihan	Teacher/master of higher rank
Shoto	Waving pines
Tai sabaki	Body movement
Tanden	Centre of the abdomen
Tokui kata	Favourite kata
Ushiro	Backward
Waza	Technique

Yoko	Side
Zanshin	Awareness

Alphabetical List of Terminology

Age empi uchi	Rising/upper elbow strike
Age uke	Upper rising block
Age zuki	Rising punch
Ashi barai	Sweeping kick
Ashi sabaki	Leg movement
Atoshi empi uchi	Downward elbow strike
Awase uke	Combination block
Awase zuki	Two armed combination punch
Bunkai	Application/analysis of kata
Choku zuki	Straight punch
Chudan	Middle level
Dachi	Stance
Dan	Rank/level (master grade)
Deshi	Student
Do	Way
Dogi	Karate uniform
Dojo	Way/place
Empi uchi	Elbow strike
Fudo dachi	Rooted stance
Fumikiri	Cutting kick
Fumikomi	Stamping kick
Gaiwan	Outside of the forearm
Gedan	Lower level
Gedan barai	Downward block
Gedan kesage	Lower level downward kick
Geri	Kick

Gohon kumite	Five-step sparring	Kakiwake uke	Wedge/push aside block
Gyaku mawashi geri	Inside roundhouse kick	Kakuto uchi	Crane head strike
Gyaku zuki	Reverse punch	Kamaete	Go into position
Hachiji dachi	Open leg stance	Kan	Hall
Haishu	Back of the hand	Kansetsu waza	Joint manipulation techniques
Haishu uke	Back of hand block	Kara	Empty
Haisoku	Instep	Kara zuki	Empty punch
Haito uchi	Ridge hand strike	Karate-do	Way of the empty hand
Haiwan	Back of the forearm		
Haiwan uchi	Back arm strike	Karateka	Person that practises karate-do
Haiwan uke	Back arm block		
Hajime	Start/begin	Kata	Pre-arranged formal exercise (forms)
Hanmi	Half body stance (hips facing sideways)		
Hara	Centre of the abdomen	Keage	Snap
		Keito uchi	Chicken head wrist strike
Heiko dachi	Parallel stance		
Heisoku dachi	Informal attention stance	Keito uke	Chicken head block
		Kekomi	Thrust
Hengetsu dachi	Half-moon stance	Kiai	Loud shout to demonstrate martial spirit
Hidari	Left		
Hikite	Withdrawing hand		
Hiraken uchi	Fore knuckle strike	Kiba dachi	Horse riding/straddle leg stance
Hiza geri	Knee kick		
Ippon	One	Kihon	Basics
Ippon ken uchi	One knuckle strike	Kihon ippon kumite	One-step sparring
Jiyu ippon kumite	Semi-freestyle sparring	Kiritsu	Stand up/rise
		Kizami zuki	Jabbing punch
Jiyu kumite	Freestyle sparring	Kokutsu dachi	Back stance
Jiyu kumite gamae	Freestyle stance	Kokyu	Breathing
Jodan	Upper-level	Kosa dachi	Cross-legged stance
Juji uke	X-block	Kosa uke	Crossing block
Jun zuki	Following punch	Koshi	Ball of the foot
Kaeshi ippon kumite	Returning one-step sparring	Kumite	Sparring
		Kyu	Rank/grade
Kage zuki	Hook punch	Kyusho	Vital points
Kakato geri	Axe kick	Maai	Distancing

217

Mae	Front	Sanchin dachi	Hour-glass stance
Mae geri keage	Front snap kick	Seiza	Sit straight
Mae geri kekomi	Front thrust kick	Sempai	One's senior
Mae tobi geri	Front jumping kick	Sensei	Instructor/master
Makiwara	Striking board	Sensei ni rei	Bow to the Sensei
Manji gamae	Vortex block in back stance	Shihan	Teacher/master of higher rank
Manji uke	Vortex block	Shihon nukite	Four finger spear hand
Mawashi empi uchi	Roundhouse elbow strike	Shiko dachi	Square stance
Mawashi geri	Roundhouse kick	Shizentai	Natural position
Mawashi zuki	Roundhouse punch	Shomen ni rei	Bow to the front
Mawate	Turn	Shoto	Waving pines
Migi	Right	Shuto uchi	Knife hand strike
Mikazuki geri	Crescent kick	Shuto uke	Knife hand block
Mokuso	Meditation	Shuwan	Underside of the forearm
Morote uke	Augmented block		
Morote zuki	Double fist punch	Sochin dachi	Strong/calm stance
Musubi dachi	Informal attention stance	Sokumen zuki	Side punch
		Sokutei	Sole of the foot
Nagashi uke	Flowing/sweeping block	Sokuto	Foot edge
		Soto ude uke	Outside forearm block
Nakadaka ken uchi	Middle finger strike		
Naiwan	Inside of the forearm	Sukui uke	Scooping block
Nami ashi	Returning wave kick	Tai sabaki	Body movement
Neko ashi dachi	Cat stance	Tanden	Centre of the abdomen
Nihon nukite	Two finger strike		
Nukite uchi	Spear hand	Tate shuto uke	Vertical knife hand block
Oi zuki	Stepping punch		
Okuri jiyu ippon	Sparring with two consecutive attacks	Tate zuki	Vertical punch
		Te	Hand
Osae uke	Pressing block	Teiji dachi	T-stance
Otagai ni rei	Bow to each other	Teisho uchi	Palm heel strike
Otoshi uke	Dropping block	Teisho uke	Palm heel block
Ren geri	Combination kicking	Tekubi	Wrist
Renoji dachi	L-stance	Tekubi kake uke	Wrist hooking block
Sanbon kumite	Three-step sparring	Tettsui uchi	Bottom fist strike
Sanbon zuki	Three level punches	Tobi geri	Jumping kick

Tokui kata	Favourite kata	Zenkutsu dachi	Front stance
Tsumasaki	Tip of the toes	Zuki	Punch
Uchi	Strike		
Uchi ude uke	Inside forearm block		
Uchi waza	Striking techniques	**Numerical System**	
Uke	Block	Ichi	1
Ura zuki	Close punch	Ni	2
Uraken uchi	Back fist strike	San	3
Ushiro	Backward	Shi	4
Ushiro empi uchi	Reverse/back elbow strike	Go	5
		Roku	6
Ushiro geri	Back kick	Shichi	7
Ushiro mawashi geri	Reverse roundhouse kick	Hachi	8
		Ku	9
Wan	Arm	Ju	10
Waza	Technique	Ju-ichi	11
Yama zuki	U-punch/mountain punch	Ju-ni	12
		Ju-san	13
Yame	Stop	Ju-shi	14
Yoi	Prepare/get ready	Ju-go	15
Yoko	Side	Ju-roku	16
Yoko empi uchi	Side elbow strike	Ju-shichi	17
Yoko geri	Side kick	Ju-hachi	18
Yoko geri keage	Side snap kick	Ju-ku	19
Yoko geri kekomi	Side thrust kick	Ni-ju	20
Yoko tobi geri	Side jumping kick	San-ju	30
Yumi zuki	Bow punch	Yon-ju	40
Zanshin	Awareness	Go-ju	50

Appendix I
Grading Syllabus

The grades up to black belt are called kyu grades and a different coloured belt identifies each grade. The number of kyu grades, and the colour of belt used for each, may differ between associations. Additionally, a system of intermediate grades is sometimes used for junior students, to help ensure a good grounding in the basic elements of karate. It should normally take between three and five years to progress through the kyu grades to shodan (1st degree black belt).

The syllabus outlined below is intended to be a guide and provides a good, structured approach to progression through the grades.

10th Kyu (Blue Belt)

Kihon

1.	Oi zuki	x 10
2.	Gedan barai	x 5 turn
3.	Oi zuki	x 5 turn
4.	Age uke	x 5 turn
5.	Uchi uke	x 5 turn
6.	Mae geri	x 5 turn

Kumite

1.	Gohon kumite: jodan	x 2

Kata

1.	Taikyoku shodan (first eight moves only)	x 2

9th Kyu (Red Belt)

Kihon

1.	Kara zuki	x 10
2.	Gyaku zuki	x 5
3.	Oi zuki	x 5 turn
4.	Age uke	x 5 turn
5.	Uchi uke	x 5 turn
6.	Soto ude uke	x 5 turn
7.	Mae geri	x 5 turn
8.	Keage (kiba dachi)	x 5 both sides
9.	Kekomi (kiba dachi)	x 5 both sides

Kumite

1.	Gohon kumite: jodan, chudan	x 2

Kata

1.	Taikyoku shodan	x 2

8th Kyu (Orange Belt)

Kihon

1.	Kara zuki	x 5
2.	Oi zuki	x 5 forward and back
3.	Age uke	x 5 forward and back
4.	Uchi uke	x 5 forward and back
5.	Soto ude uke	x 5 forward and back
6.	Shuto uke	x 5 forward and back
7.	Mae geri	x 5 turn
8.	Keage (kiba dachi)	x 5 both sides
9.	Kekomi (kiba dachi)	x 5 both sides

Kumite

1.	Gohon kumite: jodan, chudan, mae geri	x 1
2.	Kihon ippon kumite: set 1	x 1 right and left

Kata

1.	Taikyoku shodan	x 1
2.	Heian shodan	x 2

7th Kyu (Yellow Belt) and Intermediate

Kihon

1.	Oi zuki	x 5 forward and back
2.	Age uke / gyaku zuki	x 5 forward and back
3.	Ude uke / gyaku zuki	x 5 forward and back
4.	Uchi uke / gyaku zuki	x 5 forward and back
5.	Shuto uke / nukite	x 5 forward and back
6.	Mae geri	x 5 turn
7.	Keage (kiba dachi)	x 5 both sides
8.	Kekomi (kiba dachi)	x 5 both sides

Kumite

1.	Gohon kumite: jodan, chudan, mae geri	x 1
2.	Sanbon kumite: jodan, chudan, mae geri	x 1 right and left
3.	Kihon ippon kumite: set 1	x 1 right and left

Kata

1.	Taikyoku shodan	x 1
2.	Heian shodan	x 1
3.	Heian nidan	x 2

6th Kyu (Green Belt) and Intermediate

Kihon

1.	Sanbon zuki	x 5 forward and back
2.	Age uke / gyaku zuki / gedan barai	x 5 forward and back
3.	Ude uke / gyaku zuki / gedan barai	x 5 forward and back
4.	Uchi uke / gyaku zuki / gedan barai	x 5 forward and back
5.	Shuto uke / mae geri (front leg) / nukite	x 5 forward and back
6.	Mae geri	x 5 turn
7.	Keage (kiba dachi)	x 5 both sides
8.	Kekomi (zenkutsu dachi)	x 5 turn
9.	Mawashi geri	x 5 turn
10.	Ren geri: mae geri jodan / chudan	x 3 turn
11.	Ren geri: mae geri chudan / jodan	x 3 turn

Kumite

1.	Sanbon kumite: jodan, chudan, mae geri	x 1 right and left
2.	Kihon ippon kumite: set 1	x 1 right and left
3.	Kihon ippon kumite: set 2	x 1 right and left

Kata

1.	Heian shodan	x 1
2.	Heian nidan	x 1
3.	Heian sandan	x 2

5th Kyu (Purple Belt) and Intermediate

Kihon

1.	Sanbon zuki	x 5 forward and back
2.	Age uke / mae geri (back leg) / gyaku zuki	x 5 forward and back
3.	Ude uke / empi (kiba dachi) / uraken	x 5 forward and back
4.	Uchi uke / kizami zuki / gyaku zuki	x 5 forward and back
5.	Shuto uke / mae geri (front leg) / nukite	x 5 forward and back

6.	Mae geri / oi zuki	x 5 turn
7.	Mae geri / gyaku zuki	x 5 turn
8.	Ren geri: mae geri chudan / jodan	x 3 turn
9.	Ren geri: mae geri / mawashi geri	x 3 turn
10.	Ren geri: mae geri / kekomi	x 3 turn

Kumite

1.	Sanbon kumite: jodan, chudan, mae geri	x 1 both sides
2.	Kihon ippon kumite: set 2	x 1 both sides
3.	Kihon ippon kumite: set 3	x 1 both sides

Kata

1.	Heian yondan	x 2
2.	Two previous kata of examiner's choice	x 1 each

4th Kyu (Purple and White Belt) and Intermediate

Kihon

1.	Sanbon zuki / mae geri / sanbon zuki	x 5 turn
2.	Age uke / mae geri / gyaku zuki / gedan barai	x 5 forward and back
3.	Ude uke / empi / uraken / gyaku zuki / gedan barai	x 5 forward and back
4.	Uchi uke (kokutsu dachi) / kizami zuki / gyaku zuki / gedan barai	x 5 forward and back
5.	Shuto uke / mae geri (front leg) / nukite	x 5 forward and back
6.	Mae geri / mawashi geri / uraken / gyaku zuki / gedan barai	x 5 turn
7.	Mae geri / kekomi / shuto uchi / gyaku zuki / gedan barai	x 5 turn
8.	Keage (kiba dachi) / gyaku zuki (zenkutsu dachi) / gedan barai (kiba dachi)	x 5 turn

Kumite

1.	Kihon ippon kumite: set 2	x 1 both sides
2.	Kihon ippon kumite: set 3	x 1 both sides
3.	Kihon ippon kumite: set 4	x 1 both sides

Kata

1.	Heian godan	x 2
2.	Two previous kata of examiner's choice	x 1 each

3rd Kyu (Brown Belt) and Intermediate

Kihon

1.	Sanbon zuki / mae geri / sanbon zuki	x 5 turn
2.	Age uke / mae geri / gyaku zuki / gedan barai	x 5 forward and back
3.	Ude uke / empi / uraken / gyaku zuki / gedan barai	x 5 forward and back
4.	Uchi uke (kokutsu dachi) / kizami zuki / gyaku zuki / gedan barai	x 5 forward and back
5.	Shuto uke / mae geri (front leg) / nukite	x 5 forward and back
6.	Mae geri / mawashi geri / uraken / gyaku zuki / gedan barai	x 5 turn
7.	Mae geri / kekomi / shuto uchi / gyaku zuki / gedan barai	x 5 turn
8.	Keage (kiba dachi) / gyaku zuki (zenkutsu dachi) / gedan barai (kiba dachi)	x 5 turn
9.	Ushiro geri	x 5 turn
10.	Face the front: mae geri / kekomi (same leg)	x 5 both sides

Kumite

1.	Sanbon kumite	x 1 both sides
2.	Kihon ippon kumite: set 5	x 1 both sides
3.	Kihon ippon kumite: two previous sets	x 1 both sides
4.	Jiyu ippon kumite: set 1	x 1 both sides

Kata

1.	Tekki shodan	x 2
2.	Three previous kata of examiner's choice	x 1 each

2nd Kyu (Brown and White Belt) and Intermediate

Kihon

1.	Sanbon zuki / mae geri / sanbon zuki	x 5 turn
2.	Age uke / mae geri / gyaku zuki / gedan barai	x 5 forward and back
3.	Ude uke / empi / uraken / gyaku zuki / gedan barai	x 5 forward and back
4.	Uchi uke (kokutsu dachi) / kizami zuki / gyaku zuki / gedan barai	x 5 forward and back
5.	Shuto uke / mawashi geri (front leg) / nukite	x 5 forward and back
6.	Mae geri / mawashi geri / uraken / gyaku zukigeri / gedan barai	x 5 turn
7.	Mae geri / kekomi / shuto uchi / gyaku zukigeri / gedan barai	x 5 turn

8. Keage (kiba dachi) / gyaku zukigeri (zenkutsu dachi) /
   gedan barai (kiba dachi)   x 5 turn
9. Ushiro geri / gyaku zuki   x 5 turn
10. Face the front: mae geri / kekomi (same leg)   x 5 both sides
11. Face the front: mae geri / mawashi geri (same leg)   x 5 both sides

Kumite
1. Kihon ippon kumite: sets 1 to 5   x 1 both sides
2. Jiyu ippon kumite: sets 1 and 2   x 1 both sides

Kata
1. Bassai dai   x 2
2. Tekki shodan   x 1
3. Three previous kata of examiner's choice   x 1 each

1st Kyu (Brown and 2 White Belt) and Intermediate

Kihon
1. Sanbon zuki / mae geri / sanbon zuki   x 5 turn
2. Age uke / mae geri / gyaku zuki / gedan barai   x 5 forward and back
3. Ude uke / empi / uraken / gyaku zuki / gedan barai   x 5 forward and back
4. Uchi uke (kokutsu dachi) / kizami zuki / gyaku zuki /
   gedan barai   x 5 forward and back
5. Shuto uke / mawashi geri (front leg) / nukite   x 5 forward and back
6. Mae geri / mawashi geri / uraken / gyaku zuki / gedan barai x 5 turn
7. Mae geri / kekomi / shuto uchi / gyaku zuki / gedan barai   x 5 turn
8. Ushiro geri / uraken / gyaku zuki   x 5 turn
9. Kekomi (front leg) / mae geri (back leg) and step forward   x 5 turn
10. Keage (kiba dachi) / gyaku zuki (zenkutsu dachi) /
    gedan barai (kiba dachi)   x 5 turn
11. Face the front: mae geri / kekomi (same leg)   x 5 both sides
12. Face the front: mae geri / mawashi geri   x 5 both sides
13. Face the front: mae geri / ushiro geri   x 5 both sides

Kumite
1. Kihon ippon kumite: sets 1 to 5   x 1 both sides
2. Jiyu ippon kumite: sets 1 to 3   x 1 both sides

Kata

1. A choice of one of the following kata: kanku dai, empi, jion, jitte, ji'in   x 2
2. Bassai dai   x 1
3. Three previous kata of examiner's choice   x 1 each

Shodan (Black Belt – 1st Dan)

Kihon

All kihon and combination techniques are performed from the freestyle position.

1. Kizami zuki / mae geri / sanbon zuki   x 5 turn
2. Age uke / mae geri / gyaku zuki / gedan barai   x 5 forward and back
3. Ude uke / empi / uraken / gyaku zuki / gedan barai   x 5 forward and back
4. Uchi uke (kokutsu dachi) / kizami zuki / gyaku zuki / gedan barai   x 5 forward and back
5. Shuto uke / mawashi geri (front leg) / nukite   x 5 forward and back
6. Mae geri / mawashi geri / uraken / gyaku zuki / gedan barai   x 5 turn and back
7. Mae geri / kekomi / shuto uchi / gyaku zuki / gedan barai   x 5 turn and back
8. Step back age uke / mawashi geri (back leg) / uraken / oi zuki   x 5 turn and back
9. Mawashi geri (front leg) / ushiro geri / uraken / gyaku zuki / gedan barai   x 5 turn and back
10. Kekomi (front leg) / step forward: mae geri / oi zuki / gyaku zuki   x 5 turn
11. Keage / kekomi (on the same leg stepping over)   x 5 forward and back
12. Face the front: mae geri / kekomi / ushiro geri   x 5 both sides

Kumite

1. Gohon kumite: jodan, chudan   x 1 each
2. Kihon ippon kumite: sets 1 to 5   x 1 both sides
3. Jiyu ippon kumite: sets 1 to 5   x 1 both sides
4. Freestyle with three consecutive people

Kata

1. A choice of one of the following kata: kanku dai, empi, jion, jitte, ji'in   x 1 high speed
        x 1 slow speed (with interpretation)

2. One other of the above kata of the examiner's choice   x 1
3. Five previous kata of examiner's choice   x 1 each

Oral Examination
Oral examination in karate-do, including Japanese terminology

Nidan (Black Belt – 2nd Dan)

Part 1

Part 1 consists of a written paper of 1,500–2,000 words on a karate-related subject of the candidate's choice (the subject to be agreed in advance). The written paper may be submitted at any time after one year from shodan grading.

Part 2

Progression to Part 2 will follow successful completion of Part 1 above. Grading will be by invitation only and a minimum of two years must have elapsed since shodan grading.

Kihon

All kihon and combination techniques are performed from the freestyle position.

1. Kizami zuki / mae geri / sanbon zuki   x 5 turn
2. Age uke / mae geri / gyaku zuki / gedan barai   x 5 forward and back
3. Ude uke / empi / uraken / gyaku zuki / gedan barai   x 5 forward and back
4. Uchi uke (kokutsu dachi) / kizami zuki / gyaku zuki /
   gedan barai   x 5 forward and back
5. Shuto uke / mawashi geri (front leg) / nukite   x 5 forward and back
6. Mae geri / mawashi geri / uraken / gyaku zuki / gedan barai x 5 turn and back
7. Mae geri / kekomi / shuto uchi / gyaku zuki / gedan barai   x 5 turn and back
8. Step back age uke / mawashi geri (back leg) / uraken / oi zuki   x 5 turn and back
9. Mawashi geri (front leg) / ushiro geri / uraken / gyaku zuki /
   gedan barai   x 5 turn and back
10. Kekomi (front leg) / step forward: mae geri / oi zuki /
    gyaku zuki   x 5 turn
11. Gyaku zuki / mae geri / mawashi geri / shuto uchi /
    gyaku zuki / gedan barai   x 5 turn
12. Keage / kekomi (on the same leg stepping over)   x 5 forward and back
13. Face the front: mae geri keage / mae geri kekomi   x 5 both sides
14. Face the front: mawashi geri   x 5 both sides
15. Face the front: mae geri / kekomi / ushiro geri / mawashi geri   x 5 both sides

Kumite

1. Kihon ippon kumite: 2 jodan, 2 chudan, 2 mae geri, 2 kekomi, 2 mawashi geri   Hidari and Migi
2. Jiyu ippon kumite: 2 jodan, 2 chudan, 2 mae geri, 2 kekomi, 2 mawashi geri, 2 kizami zuki, 2 gyaku zuki, 2 ushiro geri   Hidari and Migi
3. Okuri jiyu ippon: 2 jodan, 2 chudan, 2 mae geri, 2 kekomi, 2 mawashi geri   Hidari and Migi
4. Freestyle with five consecutive people

Kata

1. Any of the following kata of the examiners choice: heian kata shodan to godan, tekki shodan, bassai dai, kanku dai, empi, jion, jitte, ji'in, gankaku, hengetsu
2 Tokui kata: tekki nidan, nijushiho, kanku sho, sochin, chinte

One of the above kata to be selected as tokui kata which is to be performed twice – at high speed, and slowly with interpretation.

   A good understanding of bunkai incorporated kyusho jutsu must be demonstrated

Oral Examination

Oral examination in karate-do, including Japanese terminology

Appendix II
History and Origins of Kata

It is believed that all of today's kata have been created from twenty-four originals, which were grouped between the three Okinawan schools of Naha-te, Tomari-te and Shuri-te. When referring to the origin of a kata, the names Gojo-ryu, Shorin-ryu and Shito-ryu may be used. Naha-te developed into Gojo-ryu (the hard and soft school), which is how it is still known today; while Shuri-te and Tomari-te merged, in the late nineteenth century, under the name Shorin-ryu (flexible pine school). It is from Shorin-ryu that Shotokan karate, one of the most widely practised styles today, has developed. Shito-ryu is a combination of the three ancient arts of Naha-te, Shuri-te and Tomari-te.

The same kata may be known by a number of different names. Most will have an original Okinawan name and a corresponding Japanese name, while some retain their original Chinese names. Japanese names were given to the kata by Sensei Funakoshi when karate was first taught Japan in the early 1900s. For political reasons, it was felt that these names would be more acceptable to the Japanese.

Sensei Funakoshi in his book *Karate-do* *Kyohan* makes mention of this change of names:

> The names of the kata have come down to us by word of mouth. Names in use in the past included pinan, seishan, naifanchi, wanshu, chinto and the like, many of which had ambiguous meanings and have led to frequent mistakes in instruction. Since karate is a Japanese martial art, there is no apparent reason for retaining these unfamiliar and in some cases unclear names of Chinese origin simply because of earlier usage. I have therefore changed those names I considered to be unsuitable after considering the figurative nature of the old masters' descriptions of the kata and my own study of them.

The list of the twenty-four original kata is as follows (where they have changed, the current names are shown in brackets):

Chinte
Chinto (Gankaku)
Ji'in
Jion
Jutte (Jitte)

Kururunfa
Kushanku (Kanku)
Lorei (Meikyo)
Matsukase (Wankan)
Naihanchi (Tekki)
Niseishi (Nijushiho)
Ouseishi (Gojushiho)
Passai (Bassai)
Saifa
Sanchin
Sanseru
Seienchin (Saipa)
Seipai
Seisan (Hengetsu)
Shisochin
Sochin
Suparumpei
Unsu
Wanshu (Enpi).

Although these kata are known to originate from the three ancient Okinawan styles, the exact origin is unknown. It is believed, however, that they can be grouped as shown in the chart below.

Shotokan Karate Kata

In Shotokan karate there are twenty-one advanced kata that emanate from sixteen of the original twenty-four. These are:

- Tekki shodan
- Tekki nidan
- Tekki sandan
- Bassai dai
- Bassai sho
- Kanku dai
- Kanku sho
- Jion
- Jitte
- Ji'in
- Enpi
- Gankaku·

Naha-te	Shuri-te only	Tomari-te only	Both Tomari-te and Shuri-te
Kururunfa	Chinte	Niseishi (Nijushiho)	Chinto (Gankaku)
Naihanchi (Tekki)	Kushanku (Kanku)	Sochin	Ji'in
Saifa	Ouseishi	Unsu	Jion
Sanchin	(Gojushiho)		Jutte (Jitte)
Sanseru	Passai (Bassai)		Lorei (Meikyo)
Seienchin (Saipa)			Matsukase
Seipai			(Wankan)
Seisan (Hengetsu)			Naihanchi (Tekki)
Shisochin			Wanshu (Enpi)
Suparumpei			

- Nijushiho
- Chinte
- Wankan
- Gojushiho dai
- Gojushiho sho
- Sochin
- Meikyo
- Unsu
- Hengetsu.

These kata are covered individually below.

Tekki
Previous names
Naihanchi
Naifanchi

Meaning
Horse riding
Iron horse

Origins
The kata is now practised in three forms, tekki shodan, nidan and sandan. The original kata was shodan, and it is to that kata that naihanchi relates. Sensei Funakoshi renamed the kata when he introduced the art to Japan from Okinawa. It is believed that Master Itosu created tekki nidan and sandan.

Naihanchi is known to have been practised since ancient times by Naha-te and Shuri-te, being influenced by Master Itosu. Sensei Kanazawa makes reference to the kata belonging to the Shuri-te style.

Bassai
Previous name
Passai

Meaning
To storm a fortress.
To storm a castle.
To penetrate a fortress.

Origins
The kata now comes in two forms, bassai dai and bassai sho. Dai is the major version, sho the minor. There are, however, many variations.

The original was bassai dai, with bassai sho being created in more recent times by Master Itosu. The exact origins of bassai dai are unknown. However, it has been established that it did not originate from Naha-te. The kata was practised by Shuri-te, and there is some evidence to suggest that it was also practised by Tomari-te.

Kanku
Previous names
Koshokun
Kushanku
Kwanku
Shankyu

Meaning
To view the heavens (kwanku).
To look at the sky (kanku).

Origins
The kata now comes in two forms, kanku dai and kanku sho. Dai is the major version, and sho the minor. The original kushanku relates to kanku dai. Kanku sho was created in more recent times by Master Itosu.

The kata originates from Shuri-te. It is believed that the Chinese Military Attaché to Okinawa, Kume Mura Kong-Shang

231

(Kushanku to the Okinawans), taught the kata under the name Kwanku to his student Tode Sakagawa. This kata was a favourite of Sensei Funakoshi who would often use it to demonstrate the art of karate.

Jion

Previous name
Jion is believed to be the kata's original name.

Meaning
Love and goodness
  Sensei Funakoshi in *Karate-do Kyohan* indicates that the kata was named after a Buddhist saint. It is also possible that it was named after a temple in China of the same name.

Origins
The origins of Jion are uncertain, but it is believed to be connected with the Jion-Je temple in China, a theory strengthened by the salutation at the start and finish. The kata is known to have been practised equally by Shuri-te and Tomari-te.

Jitte

Previous name
Jutte

Meaning
Ten hands or ten techniques (implying that, when mastered, one is as effective as ten men).
  Temple hands
  A jitte is also a hand weapon used in Okinawan martial arts.

Origins
Thought to be a kata from Tomari-te, although it is also known to have been practised by Shuri-te. The salutation at the start and finish of the kata suggests Chinese origins and, like jion, may have been practised at the Jion-Je temple. This is reinforced by reference to the name meaning 'temple hands'.

Ji'in

Previous name
Shokyo

Meaning
Love and shadow

Origins
Thought to be from Tomari-te, although it is also known to have been practised by Shuri-te. The kata is believed to have originated from China. This is reinforced by the Chinese salutation 'jiai no kamae' at the start and finish of the kata. Sensei Funakoshi referred to the kata as shokyo.

Enpi

Previous name
Wanshu

Meaning
Flight of a swallow.

Origins
The kata was practised by Master Itosu and is believed to originate from Shuri-te.

Gankaku

Previous name
Chinto

Meaning
Fighting towards the east.
Crane on a rock (due to the one-legged stance which resembles the sight of a crane poised on a rock about to strike out at its prey).

Origins
The originator of the kata was believed to be Chinto, a Chinese military attaché, after whom the kata was named. It is known to have been practised by both Tomari-te and Shuri-te. Chin may also relate to a Chinese technique for attacking the vital points.

Nijushiho

Previous name
Niseshi

Meaning
Twenty-four moves (or steps)
It could also relate to twenty-four vital points that the kata maps.

Origins
The exact origins of the kata are unknown, although it is known to have been practised by Tomari-te. Sensei Kanazawa states that various parts of the kata are similar to unsu and, like sochin, may have been created by Ankichi Aragaki. Sensei Nakayama writes of being taught this kata by Kenwa Mabuni, the founder of the Shito-ryu karate school.

Chinte

Previous name
Shoin

Meaning
Strange hand
Chinese hands
Incredible hands

Origins
The word Chin may relate to a Chinese technique for attacking the vital points. Therefore, the kata could be described as the technique for attacking the vital points. Its name 'Chinese hands' further strengthens the connection with China. This name may have been given to the kata following its import into Okinawa from China. Sensei Funakoshi referred to the kata as shoin, but it is not known where he obtained this name. It is believed to have been passed down through Shuri-te.

Wankan

Previous names
Shiofu
Hito
Okan
Matsukase

Meaning
King's crown

Origins
The origin of this kata is through Matsumora to Tomari-te. It has been adopted by both Shotokan and Shito-ryu, although there is a great difference between the two versions.

Gojushiho

Previous names
Ouseishi
Useshi
Hotaku

Meaning
Fifty-four moves.
Sensei Funakoshi referred to the kata as hotaku because of its resemblance to a woodpecker hitting the bark of a tree with its sharp beak.

Origins
The kata is believed to have developed through Shuri-te and been taught to Sensei Funakoshi by Master Itosu. Sensei Kenwa Mabuni, the creator of Shito Ryu, perfected the kata and called it useshi. The kata comes in two forms: gojushiho dai and gojushiho sho, dai being the major version, and sho the minor.

Sochin

Previous name
Hakko

Meaning
Old man fighting
Preserve the peace
Strength and calm

Origins
It is believed to have been passed down through Ankichi Aragaki who has links with both Shuri-te and Tomari-te.

Meikyo

Previous name
Rohai
Lorei

Meaning
Mirror of the soul
Clean mirror
Cleaning a mirror

Origins
The kata is known to have been practised by both Tomari-te and Shuri-te.

Unsu

Previous name
Believed to be the kata's original name.

Meaning
Separating or parting of the clouds.

Origins
Sensei Kanazawa makes reference to the kata belonging to the Niigaki style. Unsu may have been practised by Tomari-te, but this is far from certain.

Hengetsu

Previous name
Seishan

Meaning
Crescent or half-moon (hengetsu), because of the circular movements when moving between stances.
Forty-one movements (seishan)

Origins
Originating from Naha-te, hengetsu is one of

234

the oldest kata. Also practised by Wado-ryu under its original Okinawan name of seishan. Hengetsu is an inner kata, where you can develop inner strength and flow of energy.

Taikyoku and Heian Kata

In addition to the advanced kata referred to above, a series of more elementary kata, the taikyoku and heian kata, were introduced in the early 1900s.

Taikyoku
Previous name
Taikyoku is the original name for this range of kata.

Meaning
First cause

Origins
The Taikyoku kata come in three forms: shodan, nidan and sandan. The three kata were created by Sensei Funakoshi, who writes about the kata in his book *Karate-do Kyohan* as follows:

> If they are practiced regularly, they will result in an even development of the body and in a sound ability to bear the body correctly. Moreover, the student who has gained proficiency in basic techniques and understands the essence of the taikyoku kata will appreciate the real meaning of the maxim, 'In karate, there is no advantage in the first attack'. It is for this reason I have given them the name taikyoku.

Heian
Previous name
Pinan

Meanings
Peaceful mind
Calm mind
Way of peace
Great peace

Origins
The heian kata were created by Master Itosu in the early 1900s. It is believed that he fashioned these on a kata he had learned from a Chinese karate exponent living in Okinawa. This kata was called chiang nan and became known as channan, which is possibly an early version of kanku dai. Elements of the five heian kata also resemble parts of tekki shodan and bassai dai. It is also possible that these provided further inspiration to Sensei Itosu.

There are five heian kata: shodan, nidan, sandan, yondan and godan. Shodan is the easiest, godan the most difficult. The kata heian nidan was originally the first of the series. Sensei Funakoshi, realizing that this kata was much harder than heian shodan, changed the order in which they are taught to that which is used today.

Sensei Funakoshi in his book *Karate-do Kyohan* states that once the five heian kata have been mastered, effective self-defence will be possible in most situations.

Sensei Funakoshi was responsible for changing the names of the kata from pinan to heian in the early 1900s to facilitate the introduction of karate from Okinawa to Japan.

Bibliography and Suggested Further Reading

Alexander, G. & Penland, K., *Bubishi Martial Art Spirit* (Yamazato Publications, 1993)

Clark, R., *Pressure-Point Fighting: A Guide to the Secret Heart of Asian Martial Arts* (Tuttle, 2000)

Funakoshi, G., *Karate-Do Kyohan* (Kodansha, 1973)

Funakoshi, G., *Karate-Do Nyumon* (Kodansha, 1988)

Funakoshi, G., *To-Te Jitsu* (Masters Publications, 1997)

George, A., *The Epic of Gilgamesh* (Penguin, 1999)

Layton, C., *Mysteries of the Martial Arts* (Kime Publishing, 1989)

McCarthy, P., *Classical Kata of Okinawan Karate* (Ohara, 1987)

McCarthy, P., *The Bible of Karate–Bubishi* (Tuttle, 1995)

Miyamoto, M., *The Book of Five Rings* (various)

Nakayama, M., *Dynamic Karate* (Ward Lock, 1966)

Tzu, S., *The Art of War* (various)

Index